John Brown Mysteries

Jean Libby, editor and compiler

Judith Cephas   Henry Organ

Louis S. Diggs   Erica Phillips

James Fisher   Eva Slezak

Hannah Geffert   Evelyn M.E. Taylor

ALLIES FOR FREEDOM

Osborne P. Anderson (1829-1872) one of John Brown's liberation army; *A Voice From Harper's Ferry* (1861)

John Brown (1800-1859) revolutionary who "carried the war into Africa"

Martin R. Delany (1812-1885) friend of John Brown; national emigrationist and self-determination leader

Frederick Douglass (1818-1895) friend of John Brown; national abolitionist and American citizenship leader

W.E.B. Du Bois (1867-1963) biographer of John Brown (1909); Founder of Niagara Movement and the NAACP; social scientist, historian

Thomas W. Henry (1794-1877) African Methodist Episcopal minister; "trusty man" to John Brown

Edna Christian Knapper (1892-1985) teacher in Chambersburg, Pennsylvania; historian

Katharine DuPre Lumpkin (1897-1988) social economist; historian

Benjamin A. Matthews, graduate of Storer College in Harpers Ferry (1909); historian

Benjamin Quarles (1904-1998) historian; *Allies for Freedom; Blacks and John Brown* (1974)

Frances Rollin [Whipper] (1845-1901) historian; biographer of Martin R. Delany

Henry David Thoreau (1817-1862) revolutionary and social philosopher; friend of John Brown; *A Plea for Captain John Brown* (1859)

PICTORIAL HISTORIES PUBLISHING COMPANY, INC.

PHI

Design and composition by Archetype Typography, Berkeley, California

Cover art by James Fisher (Jimica Akinloye Kenyatta)

Pictorial Histories Publishing Company
713 South Third Street West
Missoula, Montana 59801

Library of Congress Catalog No. 99-70466

ISBN 1-57510-059-2

Table of Contents, List of Maps

Section 3: Looking for John Brown

John Brown Mysteries
Purpose and Introduction

JOHN BROWN MYSTERIES are the events of the raid on Harper's Ferry, Virginia, in October 1859, in Africentric perspective. It is a collaboration by authors who are educators and community history activists, based upon more than twenty years of research, exhibition, and publications on John Brown and Africans in America.

The research we present is counter to the prevailing textbook view that slaves refused to fight with Brown in support of their liberty, and that he might have won the battle of Harpers Ferry had they not been cowards. They have ignored the demography of the immediate area, as well as the history of the armory that Brown captured, but did not intend to hold. At least fifty local Africans in Virginia came to support Brown without previous notice. At least five of them died. Many, farther away on both sides of the Potomac and Shenandoah Rivers, left for freedom, while others were arrested for conspiracy to continue the insurrection. Yet Americans continue to hold the belief that Brown marched into Harpers Ferry with a grandiose and ill-founded plan of slave rebellion involving no more than a small, hastily gathered band and still, somehow, sparked the Civil War.

Evidence of Africans in rebellion with John Brown has been overlooked. Denial served the need of the slave society to limit the insurrection, and to propagandize that bondage was preferred by the enslaved. Brown realized he had put the local people in terrible danger by failing to "get the ball open," as he stated at his capture. At least one local slave was killed in jail within a week following the raid. Brown and the other raiders were not trying to save their own lives. Those had been freely pledged to the cause of ending slavery.

The most amazing coverup is of a mass liberation that did begin near Harpers Ferry, and continued, with large numbers of fugitive families. This is charted from the census records of fugitives in 1860. The path of the fugitives is amazing. It follows the route of the hostages taken by Brown's army. John Brown destabilized slavery in this section of Virginia just as he did in Kansas and Missouri the previous winter. It is not evident whether John Brown himself knew what he had accomplished when he was hanged on December 2nd, 1859.

Photo of an African Virginian "of the unregenerate type" in Harry H. Johnston, *The Negro in the New World* (1910).

(Courtesy The Library of the University of North Carolina at Chapel Hill.)

We use the term "Africans" for both enslaved and free people in the United States in 1859, rather than "African Americans", because Africans is the way people identified themselves. The African Methodist Episcopal Church, Free African Society, the African Clarkson Society, an African Grove Theatre in New York, all flourished in the early 1800s; by midcentury, the African Civilization Society founded by Rev. Henry Highland Garnet, and the African Commission founded by Dr. Martin R. Delany were in full swing.

The *Dred Scott v. Sandford* decison of the United States Supreme Court (1857) declared that no person of African descent, free or enslaved, born in this country, could be a citizen. Voting was racially prohibited in many states where slavery was illegal long before 1857, and the franchise a major topic of conventions and petitions. Therefore, Africans in the United States were a stateless people except when relating to the ancestral homeland until the guarantee of citizenship by the 14th Amendment in 1867, and the 15th Amendment, voting rights for black men, in 1870.

This 1862 image of an African woman born on the Lee family plantations in Virginia provides an example of a "servant", a supposedly privileged group seldom called "slaves" by the gentry. One woman at the Washington farm in Halltown attempted suicide following Brown's raid because her free husband ran to join Brown's army, and was killed in the early hours of the fighting. Brown chose Sunday night to begin the raid because local Africans were allowed to move fairly freely between plantations for family visits.

African self-liberation began before John Brown became a black nationalist. The formation of independent communities of free persons of color before the Civil War — in Maryland, western Pennsylvania, even Jefferson County, Virginia — provided the base John Brown wanted for his army and the leadership for a self-determining state or nation of freedmen. We find evidence of these early communities by the historic presence of independent churches and congregations, lodges, and delegates to the Black Conventions of the 1850s. That is where John Brown looked for them, too.

Publication of the mysteries is based upon new research motivated by the discovery of two Harpers Ferry rifles, a shotgun, a pistol, and a fowling piece in the attic of a home of black community leaders of the 19th century in Catonsville, Maryland. All these weapons were named in documents as given to local Africans during the raid. Hannah Geffert interviewed the heirs, and writes "The Guns of October" with intriguing questions about a brass "W" on one of the long guns. Could it be one taken from Lewis Washington on the night of October 16, 1859, last seen in the hands of a "negro on the Maryland side of the Potomac River?"

We sought the assistance of Doug Wicklund, curator of the National Firearms Museum of the National Rifle Association, in dating the guns, which primarily came from Civil War veterans in the Woodland family of Maryland. With research assistance from Julie DeMatteis of the Baltimore County Public Library in Catonsville, the family was examined in their archives records, including military pensions. We can see origins of the Woodland family in African tradition of clan formation, and their subsequent community leadership a result of their self-determination as a family identity. The present owners of the weapons, Charles Cephas, and his mother, Lucille Woodland Cephas, continue that tradition in the present day by sharing the story of their heirlooms that honor John Brown.

Our mysteries document and corroborate statements about local Africans by Osborne P. Anderson, who was the only member of Brown's original army to successfully escape from the battle on October 17, 1859. Like his captain and comrades in prison in Virginia in 1859, Anderson had to mask the presence of local people to save their lives when he wrote his account *A Voice From Harper's Ferry* in 1861. "The Slaves Who Fought With John Brown" is revised from *Black Voices from Harpers Ferry*, which Jean Libby published in 1979.

We are aware that evidence, whether written or oral, that places Africans in the center of an historical event is often discounted among white historians, no matter how liberal they profess to be. The historical place for

Africans in America is on the sidebars, as victims. However, the primary sources we cite are from local whites describing militant action by the local blacks. It is clear that these whites – no matter if a Congressman, slaveholder, or the president of the B & O Railroad — are ignored or downplayed if their stories do not fit the stereotype of submissive and cowardly, slaves.

So who is correct? This is an historical dilemma that only can be resolved by looking straight at "the big lie," slavery. The institution required slaveholders to justify slavery and to defend it, while living off the labor and fertility of the captives. In the analysis of Malcolm X: "He hated his master" is key to historical evidence of African people acting upon that hate, to the process of captivity and cultural genocide that Europeans called slavery.

To make the case for self-defense and revolution, we are bound by traditional rules of scholarly historical evidence. These rules require at least two independent primary sources in agreement that an event or circumstance actually occurred, or could have occurred, in the way that is described. We found deeds, wills, local newspaper accounts, and the indictment list of eleven named individuals, called property, with whom John Brown "conspired to rebel, not having the fear of God in their eyes . . . . and at the instigations of the devil." We found that these eleven were not alone in rebellion, and some of the "diverse other slaves to the jurors unknown" were documented as well.

Primary and secondary references in this book are annotated to make this evidence plain and accessible and to encourage further study. We seek communication to continue solving the mysteries:

allies7@AlliesforFreedom.org.

John Brown's experiences as an Underground Railroad activist since his childhood in Ohio, then in western Pennsylvania, New York, and Kansas made him grow in militant perspective. It is among African emigrationists who were strategizing self-determining polities as well as self-defense organizations where his militant liberation ideas gained most acceptance.

The chart of the African Commission connections, later Civil War units, and leadership in Reconstruction governments among the delegates to the Chatham Convention in 1858 buttresses the emigrationist spirit of these leaders with John Brown. James Fisher, whose African name is Jimica Akinloye Kenyatta, writes "The Nationalist and the Revolutionary: Martin R. Delany and John Brown" with this perspective. Mr. Fisher created the cover for *John Brown Mysteries*, and the Africentic view of Martin Delany, whose varied talents were aimed toward an African resolution of the ruptures of European slavery.

Our group name is taken from the title, *Allies for Freedom; Blacks and John Brown*, written by historian Benjamin Quarles in 1974. He offered personal encouragement to scholars, whether traditionally affiliated or not, to continue researching African involvement with John Brown, using historical documentation.

ALLIES FOR FREEDOM

Red — blood drawn and dropped by
Black — people as we struggle to defend the
Green — fields of mother Africa

Marcus Garvey

"Allies for Freedom" and the impetus for this book began in 1998, when a middle school resource specialist in Maryland, Judith Grievous Cephas, contacted the editor in online discussion on the role of Frances Watkins Harper and John Brown, and asked if there was interest in some Harpers Ferry rifles found in an attic in Catonsville. Three longtime associates in research — Jean Libby of California, Jim Fisher and Hannah Geffert of West Virginia — gathered at Harpers Ferry to assist in family research related to Storer College, the historical wellspring for African Americans in the leadership of Jefferson County, West Virginia. We were ably guided by Gwen Roper of the National Park Service at Harpers Ferry, the daughter of Mr. and Mrs. Russell Roper of Charles Town, who have provided oral history interviews to researchers over the past twenty five years. Another West Virginian, author and family researcher Evelyn M.E. Taylor of Jefferson County, found many free Africans of 1859, as well as those enslaved, in the churches which are still active in the area today.

We invited Louis S. Diggs, historian of African American settlements in Baltimore County, to contribute. He has been a mainstay of information and connections. The African American Collection librarian at Enoch Pratt Library in Baltimore, Eva Slezak, traced the locations of independent African congregations and organizations in Baltimore in 1859, for her original map; journalist Erica Phillips, a graduate student at York University in Canada, volunteered to go to present-day Chatham to look for John Brown. She learned of the project through a query on the Humanities Net African American discussion forum.

Henry P. Organ, a civil rights activist in California, developed the *dramatis personae* of the watershed meeting of August, 1859: John Brown, Frederick Douglass, and Shields Green. Jean Libby was editor of the newsletter of the Midpeninsula Congress of Racial Equality (CORE) in the mid1960s when Henry Organ was the branch chair. He helped in creating her work on John Brown and black nationalism in the form of a narrated slide program, which became an educational videotape produced by the University of California, Berkeley: *Mean To Be Free: John Brown's Black Nation Campaign* (1986, with Roy Thomas). This was done in the company of the eminent scholar, the late Professor St. Clair Drake of Stanford University, whose words of advice included the admonition to include the Final Address of John Brown to the Court, November 2, 1859 in any study on Brown.

Among John Brown's New England contemporaries, the most revolutionary was Henry David Thoreau. A present-day Chicago illustrator, Josh Macphee, makes "Celebrate People's History" posters of the birth days of revolutionary Americans to distribute their ideals freely and widely.

Among our research discoveries is a cousin relationship between two of the men in Brown's original army, Lewis Leary and John Copeland, with Hiram Revels, the first United States senator of African descent. His brother Rev. Willis Revels, who was a doctor as well as minister in Indiana in the Civil War era, deserves historical recognition. This research was enabled by the interest of library specialist Rhonda L. Williams at the Cumberland County Information Center in Fayetteville, North Carolina (the home place of the Learys and the Revels), to dig deep and follow leads. She aided the connection of North Carolinian James H. Harris, a leader in Brown's Chatham Convention and the Civil War, and his return to be a legislator in his original home, along with John Leary, the brother of Lewis.

The presentation of John Brown mysteries is done in many graphics, designed to tell the story in their own way. These were prepared by Scott Perry of Archetype Typography, a service for progressive publishers in Berkeley, California.

We are inspired by the movements of Africans to free themselves and to replicate the traditions of their West African societies in the Americas. These maroon groups are celebrated in Brazil and the Caribbean among descendants today. They were present in colonial North America and the United States, too, and greatly influenced the strategies of leadership of militant abolitionists and nationalists such as Martin R. Delany and John Brown. Their skills lay not as much in military tactics as in recruitment of slaves through their absolute commitment to plans that would restore self-determination to the Africans.

We are inspired by Professor Angela Y. Davis of the University of California at Santa Cruz, who urges progressive scholars to collaborate in presenting their research and ideas. We are inspired by the greatest disciple of W.E.B. Du Bois, historian and activist Herbert Aptheker, who documented the organization within the African population known by John Brown: "The ancient cliche that American Negro slavery was characterized by placidity is a colossal hoax . . ."

The meaning of John Brown to Africans in America takes many forms. One of the most outstanding was made by the Rev. Jesse Jackson on national television in 1984. Invoking a panoply of black heroes, he paused on the name of John Brown and said, "A lie cannot live forever!".

> *Jean Libby*
> *Hannah Geffert*
> *James Fisher*

The banner of *The Mystery,* published
in Pittsburgh, Pennsylvania in the 1840s
by Martin R. Delany. (Courtesy Jim
Surkamp)

Marching to a Monument for Freedom

Remembering the Raid: 50th annual state convention of the West
Virginia NAACP, August 1994. The group is led by Ranger Gwen
Roper of the National Park Service.

JOHN BROWN'S DAY started early. At six in the morning his admirers left the site of
the convention, Storer College, a [Free Will] Baptist-controlled school founded in
1867 for blacks, to make a pilgrimage to the brick-walled fire engine house (John
Brown's fort) a mile away. As they neared their destination they formed a procession,
single file, led by Owen M. Waller, a physician from Brooklyn. Defying stone and stub-
ble, Waller took off his shoes and socks and walked barefoot as if treading on holy
ground. Halting outside the enginehouse, the pilgrims listened to prayer, followed by
remarks from Richard T. Greener . . . Harvard's first black graduate and former dean
of the Howard University Law School, Greener was gifted in speech and handsomely
magisterial in appearance. Forgoing a formal oration punctuated by the Latin phrases
he knew so well, Greener recited his personal recollections of John Brown and the excitement in Boston and elsewhere immediately following the raid on Harpers Ferry.
Closing with an incident more contemporary, Greener related that during his recent
tenure as American consul at Vladivostok he had heard the Russian troops burst into
the song, "John Brown's body lies a-moldering in the grave."

Benjamin Quarles, *Allies for Freedom*
on the Niagara Meeting at Harpers Ferry, 1906 led by W.E.B. Du Bois

This pilgrimage included the widow of Lewis Leary, killed in the 1859 raid (seated left center, directly under umbrella). Mary Leary and her infant daughter were assisted by African friends of John Brown, one of whom, Charles Langston, married her after the Civil War. Their grandson was the poet, Langston Hughes, born in 1902. "John Brown's Fort" was, at this time, on the Murphy Farm in Harpers Ferry, where it was reconstructed by Kate Fields. (Courtesy Hannah N. Geffert)

The American Legion of veterans in Charles Town in 1929 took the name of Shields Green and John Copeland, hanged on December 16, 1859, for attempting to end slavery with John Brown. This group includes the father of the president of the regional NAACP, Edward D. Tolbert, and Reginald R. Ross, whose father escaped from Loudon County at the time of John Brown's raid. Note the signator of the Department Adjutant: it is Boyd B. Stutler, who amassed the largest collecton of materials on Brown, now at West Virginia University in Morgantown. (Certificate courtesy James Tolbert, Chares Town)

What was John Brown's Plan?

"SIR, THE ANGEL of the Lord will camp around me," said John Brown with stern eyes when the timid foretold his doom. With a steadfast almost superstitious faith in his divine mission, the old man had walked unscathed out of Kansas in the fall of 1856, two years and a half before the slave raid into Missouri related the last chapter. In his mind lay a definitely matured plan for attacking slavery in the United States in such a way as would shake its very foundations. The plan had been long forming, and changing in shape from 1828, when he proposed a Negro school in Hudson, until 1859 when he finally fixed on Harper's Ferry. At first he though to educate Negroes in the North and let them leaven the lump of slaves. Then, moving forward a step, he determined to settle in a border state and educate slaves openly or clandestinely and send them out as emissaries. As gradually he became acquainted with the great work and wide ramifications of the Underground Railroad, he conceived the idea of central depots for running off slaves in the inaccessible portions of the South, and he began studying mountains, and more especially, the great struggling heights of the Alleghanies, which swept from his Pennsylvania home down to the swamps of Virginia,

Carolina, and Georgia. His Kansas experiences suggested for a time the southwest pathway by the swamps of the Red and Arkansas Rivers, but this was a passing thought; he soon reverted to the great spur of the Alleghanies.

W. E. Burghardt Du Bois
John Brown, 1909

African American intellectual, founder of the Niagara Movement, then the National Association for the Advancement of Colored People; Du Bois envisioned a pan-Africa, removing European colonialism with diasporan leadership. He became a citizen of Ghana in 1961, at age ninety-three.

W.E. Burghardt Du Bois
Social Scientist

11

Frances Rollin Whipper, biographer of Martin R. Delany

Major Martin R. Delany, in 1866, faced a discouraging problem in a way that was characteristic of his relationship with young African intellectual women: he gave 21-year old Frances Rollin a job, entrusting her with writing his biography. Delany was a prolific writer and editor, but his collection of papers of more than twenty years burned that year in a fire at Wilberforce University, the African Methodist Episcopal seminary in Ohio. He needed to replace them as nearly as he could, while at the same time working as a Sub-Assistant Commissioner with the Freedmen's Bureau in attempting to gain the promised lands of victory over the slaveholders for Africans in South Carolina. His recent Civil War service as major in the 104th Infantry, United States Colored Troops, made this biographical information critical to establish.

Frances Rollin was the oldest daughter of a Black Confederate, a merchant and slaveholder who was descended from both light and dark-skinned Haitian immigrants. The well-educated and traveled William Rollin placed Frances in the Quaker Institute for Colored Youth in Philadelphia in 1859. She lived with the African Methodist Episcopal family of Morris Brown, a free minister who had escaped from Charleston after he was suspected of being in conspiracy with Denmark Vesey in 1822. She was then fourteen, and returned to her family in Charleston after the Civil War, when she was twenty. She went to Hilton Head to become a teacher of freed people, and it was there she met Delany.

The first African woman historian was turned down by a publisher to whom William Lloyd Garrison had sent the manuscript, *Life and Public Services of Martin R. Delany*. She found another Boston publisher, Lee and Shepherd, who published the book in the fall of 1868, with a male name, Frank Rollin. She then married an African (American), William Whipper of New York.

Frances Rollin Whipper
Historian, 1868
(Leigh Whipper Collection,
Schomburg Research Center
for Black Culture, NYPL)

The Convention, when assembled, consisted of Captain John Brown, his son Owen, eleven or twelve of his Kansas followers, all young white men, enthusiastic and able, and probably sixty or seventy colored men, whom I brought together.

His plans were made known to them as soon as he was satisfied that the assemblage could be confided in, which conclusion he was not long in finding, for with few exceptions the whole of these were fugitive slaves, refugees in her Britannic majesty's dominion. His scheme was nothing more than this: To make Kansas, instead of Canada, the terminus of the Underground Railroad; instead of passing off the slave to Canada, to send him to Kansas, and there test, on the soil of the United States territory, whether or not the right to freedom would be maintained.

"He stated that he had originated a fortification so simple, that twenty men, without the aid of teams or ordnance, could build one in a day that would defy all the artillery that could be brought to bear against it. How it was constructed he would not reveal, and none knew it except his great confidential officer, Kagi (the secretary of war in his contemplated provisional government) a young lawyer of marked talents and singular demeanor."

Major Delany stated that he had proposed, as a cover to the change in the scheme, as Canada had always been known as the terminus of the Underground Railroad, and pursuit of the fugitive was made in that direction, to call it the Subterranean Pass Way, where the initials would stand S.P.W., to note the direction in which he had gone when not sent to Canada. He further stated that the idea of Harper's Ferry was never mentioned, or even hinted in that convention.

Had such been intimated, it is doubtful of its being favorably regarded. Kansas, where he had battled so valiantly for freedom, seemed the proper place for his vantage-ground, and the kind and condition of men for whom he had fought, the men with whom to fight. Hence the favor which the scheme met of making Kansas the terminus of the Subterranean Pass Way, and there fortifying with these fugitives against the Border slaveholders, for personal liberty, with which they had no right to interfere. Thus it is clearly explained that it was no design against the Union, as the slaveholders and their straps interpreted the movement, and by this means would anticipate their designs . . .

Martin Robison Delany
Nationalist

The 1848 Colored National Convention (Frederick Douglass, President) passed an "Address to the Colored People of the United States" stating their obligation to those enslaved: "It is more than a mere figure of speech to say, that we are, as a people, chained together. We are one people — one in general complexion, one in common degradation, one in popular estimation —. As one rises, all must rise, and as one falls, all must fall."

Address to Storer College, Harpers Ferry, 1881

With eighteen men he overpowered a town of nearly three thousand souls. With these eighteen men he rallied fifty slaves to his standard, and made prisoners of an equal number of the slaveholding class. . . .

If John Brown did not end the war that ended slavery, he did at least begin the war that ended slavery. When we look over the dates, places, and men for which this honor is placed, we shall find that not Carolina, but Virginia, not Fort Sumter, but Harpers Ferry and the arsenal, not Colonel Anderson, but John Brown began the war that ended American slavery and made this a free Republic.

And until this blow was struck the prospects for freedom were dim, shadowy, and uncertain. The irrepressible conflict was one of worthy words, votes, and compromise. When John Brown stretched forth his arms the sky was filled, the time for compromise was gone, the armed host of freedom to face . . . over the chasm of a broken Union, and the clash of arms was at hand. The South staked all on getting possession of the Federal government. And failing to do that drew the sword of rebellion and thus made her own and not Brown's the Lost Cause of the century.

Frederick Douglass, Editor
Julia Griffiths, *Autographs
for Freedom*, 1854

" . . . it was his [John Brown's] peculiar doctrine that a man has a perfect right to interfere by force with the slaveholder, in order to rescue the slave. I agree with him. They who are continually shocked by slavery have some right to be shocked by the violent death of the slaveholder, but such will be more shocked by his life than by his death. I shall not be forward to think him mistaken in his method who quickest succeeds to liberate the slave."
                                                    — Henry David Thoreau

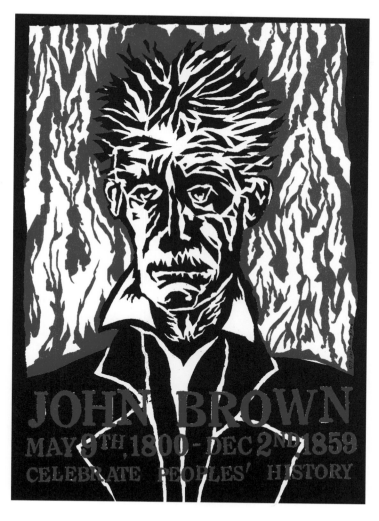

"Celebrate People's History"
Created by Josh Macphee for public distribution
P.O. Box 476971, Chicago, IL 60647

The Slaves Who Fought With John Brown

AND THE AFORESAID, being a free person, on the sixteenth and seventeenth day of the month of October, in the year Eighteen hundred and fifty nine . . . not having the fear of God before his eyes, but being moved and seduced by the instigations of the Devil, did maliciously, wilfully and feloniously conspire with certain slaves of the county and commonwealth aforesaid, to wit: negro slaves Jim, Sam, Mason, and Catesby, the slaves of Lewis W. Washington, and negro slaves Henry, Levi, Ben, Jerry, Phil, George, and Bill, the slaves of John W. Allstadt, and with each of said slaves severally, to rebel and make insurrection against their said masters respectively, and against the authority of the Constitution and Laws of the said Commonwealth of Virginia.[1]

Joseph Cermak, *Dejiny Obscanske Valky,* 1889

---

1. Indictment against John Brown in the Virginia courts. The treason for which he was convicted was against Virginia, not the United States.

One was a free man, visiting his wife. He hurried to the fight, and was the first on Brown's side to die. Jim, his companion, was clubbed to death in the Shenandoah River. Ben, saved from lynching at that moment, then died in jail within the week, of "pneumonia and fright." Mason fought for his freedom with a double-barreled shotgun, then buried it in Maryland for safekeeping. He spent six hours in the company of Captain John Cook and a hostage schoolteacher listening to antislavery arguments while the guns thundered across the Potomac River.

The report of the local commander, Robert W. Baylor, cites four more deaths of "insurgents" than the historical total of ten, all of whom cannot be attributed to the John Brown's original army — Col. Robert E. Lee had two more bodies in his report than historians acknowledge.

These were the anonymous "slaves," who become more real as their names leap from the pages of wills, newspapers, the Jefferson County Death Register, 1859. Some who helped were legally free persons named and counted on the census. What relationship did John Brown have with them during the raid, and thereafter. How was he able to help save lives when he was losing his own?

Jefferson County, Virginia was unique in its demography in comparison to nearby counties to the south, which had proportionally more slaves to whites, and directly north, in Maryland, which had proportionally more free Africans to both whites and the enslaved.

Virginia law (after 1806) required manumitted persons, those who individually purchased legal freedom, to leave the state within a year after this was accomplished, unless they made a direct arrangement through the legislature, essentially posting a bond. This created descriptions of "free slaves," and "slaves, living as free," often when individuals had absentee slaveholders.

This law caused rupture in families when some were still enslaved. Dangerfield Newby left after manumission from his father, the slaveholder, who moved west with his African family. Newby joined John Brown's army when the purchase of his wife and children from another slaveholder was denied when he returned for them in the summer of 1859. They were sold into Louisiana after Newby died fighting with John Brown.

Martin Delany had an enslaved father in Martinsburg when his free mother and the freeborn children were forced to leave the state for the crime of learning to read in 1819. Together, the family earned the money to purchase Samuel Delany, and he joined them in Chambersburg, Pennsylvania — a free state. Chambersburg had an economic and social rewith western Maryland (a slave state) and what would become West Virginia, the locality of the raid.

The important distinction in the cases of Delany and Newby was the condition of the mother. Children born of free women were free, even if the father was enslaved; those of enslaved women were in bondage for their lives, even if the mother was promised freedom at a later date.

An especially oppressive practice was the dower right of white women to the children of enslaved women in perpetuity. Those in that group could not purchase freedom. They were the wealth of aristocratic women, who usually did not inherit land if they had sons or brothers.

This was the situation of the slaves of George Turner, the slaveholder pursuing his bondsmen who had joined John Brown's men. Turner was killed at the Rifle Works early Monday afternoon of the raid. At least one of those enslaved to him died in the Rifle Works battle as well. Three eyewitness accounts attest to more deaths in the Shenandoah River than history texts later acknowledge.

George Turner, who was dead in 1860, had three fugitive slaves listed next to his name in the Jefferson County Slave Schedule, ages twenty and three (females) and sixteen (male). In 1850 he held nine people in bondage, three of whom were young men in their twenties. On December 27, 1859, George Turner's mother (he was unmarried) sold her "life interest" in the personal estate of George to her second son, William. There were no adult males in George Turner's estate inventory. The young women of childbearing age and their healthy children, ages infant to thirteen, were valued at a total of $250.[2] John Brown destabilized slavery by devaluing the price of rebellious slaves.

The size of the plantations of the kidnapped slaveholders, Lewis Washington and John Allstadt, is revealing of the demography of slavery in Jefferson County. There were twelve persons enslaved to Allstadt in 1860, of whom only five were adult men. Lewis Washington held eight adult men in slavery in 1860. The total of 4,014 enslaved in the county in 1860 (4,431 in 1850) were greatly dispersed among the white population of over 10,000.

The demography of the towns of Harpers Ferry and Bolivar (the hill above) is equally striking. The ratio of white over black was 10:1, and the total population — which increased slightly between 1850 and 1860 — was

---

2. Dower right to Lucy L. Turner 14 March, 1845. George Turner's estate was appraised on Dec. 5, 1859, by Richard Bushrod Washington and others. *Jefferson County Deeds and Wills 1859-1862*, p. 39.

accurately stated by Frederick Douglass as "three thousand souls." The free African population in town was characterized by family dwellings, small businesses, and laborers. They worked in ancillary occupations but were not allowed by the white workers to work in the armory and arsenal. The majority, free and slave, were women and children.

We believe the free and enslaved Africans in Virginia who were close enough to give Brown support (before he was closed in by the white militia by noon on the following day) numbered about 150 adults (men and women) in the two towns and nearby farms and mills. Among these, from 20 to 30 persons quickly joined, and were armed by Brown. They stopped and guarded the eastbound passenger train, assisted the raiders in locating slaveholders, and gave other guidance in town. These local Africans helped Osborne Anderson and Albert Hazlett escape from the battlefield area and across the Potomac River at nightfall, after Brown was surrounded. This hypothesis is buttressed by a concentration of fugitives at the Engle farm (see map), adjacent to the point where the pair "find" a rowboat.

Further support after the raid came near Charles Town, eight miles away. The barns of all of the jurors of John Brown's trial were burned — a time-honored signal of revolution that went unanswered from the outside. George Turner's barn was burned on the day of Brown's execution, and many animals found poisoned. An equal number joined in Maryland, stopping the westbound train, and carrying the rebellion as far as Carroll County.[3] Add to these numbers the eleven named in the indictments (ten adult men and one man child) and three men from George Turner's, the slaveholder killed in the fighting.

Those who were known — the nine remaining alive of the eleven named in the indictments — carried the largest burden. With John Brown's defeat, they had to maintain a servile position to save their lives. John Brown knew this when he refused assistance from his Kansas friends to escape by military attack. "There has been enough killing, and many more would die." Most painful of all, he referred to the local men who had joined him in prisoner terms — "the slaves we took about the Ferry." The Liberator would not use this language without a deep sense of the danger in which he had placed them.

---

3. *Baltimore Sun* Oct., 1859 describes a group of families at "Dr. Butler's" preparing with horses and carriages to "stampede" to freedom. Five were arrested.

Chronology of the Raid

May, 1858 Constitutional Convention for the Oppressed People of the United States held in Canada; attended by African emigration leaders.

August, 1858 Plans held in abeyance because an Englishman wants control; white financial supporters panic. Brown returns to Kansas

December, 1858 – January, 1859 Brown and his core army leaders rescue twelve slaves in Missouri, killing a slaveholder. They are aided and welcomed as heroes throughout the midwest.

July, 1859 Brown ships weapons to Chambersburg, Pennsylvania; boards white army with Mrs. Ritner, black army with Mr. and Mrs. Watson; moves to Kennedy Farm near Sharpsburg, Maryland; brings daughters to give the appearance of normalcy while bringing in men.

August, 1859 Frederick Douglass and Shields Green meet with Brown in Chambersburg; Douglass decides not to participate because it seems certain to fail; Shields Green, fugitive and defender, chooses to "stay with the old man.".

September-October, 1859 The arrival of all twenty-one young men who will form the army of liberation; suspicion in neighborhood changes planned date from October 24 to October 16.

October 16, 1859 "Men, get on your arms. We will proceed to the Ferry." Eighteen proceed across the bridge to take the town, wounding a watchman and killing the baggage-master (an African man, Haywood Shepherd).

October 17, 1859 Six men in Brown's army capture pre-selected slaveholders Lewis Washington and John Allstadt, liberating eleven slaves who wish to join. Osborne Anderson receives a sword owned by President George Washington as a token of power to a black man; also take two antique pistols, a shotgun, and a fowling rifle. All return to town except Shields Green and Lewis Leary, who are notifying local Africans at George Turner's; find supporters guarding the stopped passenger train; all are armed by Brown and Anderson with weapons from the arsenal. Wagons (one hijacked) are loaded with arms and men, cross the Potomac River to Maryland, to transfer arms from Kennedy farmhouse to a schoolhouse closer to the river and canal. Terence Byrne taken hostage in Maryland and Africans join the group. Passenger train going east is allowed to proceed; Conductor Phelps reaches live telegraph lines at Monocacy at 7 a.m. His reports of armed insurrection are unbelieved at first.

October 17, midmorning Schoolhouse is commandeered and children sent home; schoolteacher aids them and returns as a hostage; recognizes a Washington bondsman (possibly Mason) and others who bring arms into the schoolhouse from the arsenal and from Kennedy farmhouse; operations at farm in

20

charge of Charles Tidd and Owen Brown; at schoolhouse in charge of John Cook Mail train going west is stopped by local Africans at Weverton, conductor and baggage-master brought to Brown, who tells them to return with message to authorities to allow no more trains to proceed east or west. B&O RR President John W. Garrett notifies militia in Frederick; by 11:30 a.m. notifies U.S. Army in Baltimore that "an insurrection is in progress at Harper's Ferry, and on the Maryland side, in which free negroes and whites are engaged." Lewis Leary and Shields Green return with local Africans from Turner's. Posting at Hall's Rifle Works on the Shenandoah River include local people from Allstadt and Turner farms, John Copeland and Lewis Leary, and John Kagi, a white of Virginia origin who is the most revolutionary, and most learned, of Brown's forces. Brown delays leaving for unknown reasons; local whites begin fighting with arms kept in reserve in hills; early battles kill local free African man visiting his wife; an armed local grocer killed by a slave.

October 17, noon   Armed and uniformed militia from Shepherdstown have reached Harpers Ferry, fight Brown's forces in the houses and streets, killing white Canadian Steward Taylor, forcing others into the engine house with hostages. Oliver Brown killed in engine house. Brown's men Aaron Stevens and Watson Brown, with white flags in the street, are badly wounded. Shields Green returns to the engine house. A railroad conductor fighting with townsmen is killed. Albert Hazlett and Osborne Anderson hide in a residence basement when Dangerfield Newby is killed and all others are trapped. At the Rifle Works, the slaveholder George Turner, pursuing his slaves, has been killed. Jim and Ben, armed and guarding near the Rifle Works (where Kagi has sent messages in vain to Brown asking him to leave) are captured. Jim is chased into the canal and clubbed to death, Ben surrenders and is nearly lynched.

October 17, 2 p.m.   Rifle Works forces are fired upon by hundreds of whites on the hill above. All attempt to swim the Shenandoah — Kagi and two local slaves are killed on the rocks, Leary is mortally wounded, and Copeland is arrested and nearly lynched. Under interrogation, Leary does not implicate any friends, says he joined in Ohio as an adventure, movement is small. Most prisoners adjacent to engine house released, and local Africans guarding them flee. Firing from engine house continues; Phil is asked by Brown to make holes in brick wall, which he does until hit by a brick dislodged by a bullet. Brown tells local slaves to stay as far from him as possible, as he is expecting to be killed. Mayor of town, Fontaine Beckham, killed from engine house while appearing to be a sniper on the water tower, but is unarmed.

October 17, 4 p.m.   Maryland militia from Frederick is on its way to Harpers Ferry when commander stops train at Monocacy Junction to wait for a cannon to accompany them; Africans in Maryland begin to disperse. John Cook leaves the schoolmaster guarded by Mason, fires from the hills, returns to Kennedy Farm to seek other whites. All have been warned by local Africans sent by

Brown they are needed in Harpers Ferry; all believe that John Brown died when they hear firing stop. Brown is surrounded in the engine house, still holding a dozen hostage slaveholders. His son Oliver is dead, Watson is badly wounded but fights on. All his men are killed or captured, (two — William Leeman and William Thompson — are then killed), leaving four of his army unwounded and about six local enslaved Africans, all from the Allstadt and Washington farms, in the engine house. Brown is surrounded by Jefferson County militia and townsmen, extends a white flag. Anderson and Hazlett see this exchange, and believe Brown has surrendered. They are able to move through town to a wooded hill, and later to a sawmill on the Potomac with the aid of a local African who may have been Joseph Blanham, a boatman living on Virginius Island. Occasional firing occurs to and from the engine house.

October 17, 8 p.m.   Troops from Frederick proceed by train across bridge, surround engine house, relieving local militia. Some sporadic firing, then a surrender parley from Brown, seeking to be placed on the Maryland side near the schoolhouse, promising to release hostages if given a head start. With arrival of Baltimore militia companies, Brown is informed he is completely surrounded. Federal marines under the command of Col. Robert E. Lee of the United States Cavalry on the Maryland side of the bridge. Cross bridge at 2 a.m.; decide to wait for daylight to attack. Maryland side raiders prepare to walk to Pennsylvania, coercing a local slave to accompany them because he knows their plans. He escapes. Local free Africans keep Virginia slaves safe for two days, when they return from Point of Rocks, Maryland. Washington remains away from Beallair "on business" for four days.

Tuesday, October 18, 8 a.m.   John Brown is captured at the engine house by J.E.B. Stuart and marines. One marine killed, three of Brown's men killed, in the fighting —Watson Brown mortally wounded. John Brown wounded with a sword. African men still firing across the Potomac River, engage troops. John Brown taken to jail in Charles Town, where Ben, already there, dies of "fright" about October 20. His mother, Arely, dies of exposure three weeks later. Surviving men are tried and sentenced to death for murder, inciting slaves to insurrection, and treason to the Commonwealth of Virginia. The African men Green and Copeland are not charged with treason because they could not be citizens. All are sentenced to hang.

Those Executed

John Brown (December 2, 1859)

Shields Green and John Copeland (December 16, 1859)

John Cook and Edwin Coppoc (December 16, 1859)

Albert Hazlett and Aaron Stevens (March 16, 1860)

"WHAT'S DEM FOOL NIGGERS FRAID ON? I'D LIKE
TER SEE ONE O' DEM FOLKS ONDERTAKE TO
CARRY ME OFF, I WOULD!"
Harper's Weekly,
November 19, 1859

THE COOK
Porte Crayon and His Cousins,
1857

The artist and writer for *Harper's Weekly*, David Hunter Strother, was related to many of the principals on the slaveholding side of John Brown's raid — the prosecuting attorney, Andrew Hunter, a major eyewitness/participant, David E. Henderson — even to J.E.B. Stuart's wife, Flora. Yet his accounts of the raid published in the ensuing weeks have been considered unbiased by historians. Known as Porte Crayon, he was well-known for his life drawings of local Africans that were detailed and reflective. He altered these images to create subhuman and cowardly faces, or drawing knives (never guns) in the hands of local slaves to be used in defending the masters.

The plantation of Lewis Washington. The slave "quarters" where local people were recruited is in the background. Note the second floor. The building at left front is a cook house.

Charlotte Fairbairn, *The Washington Homes of Jefferson County, West Virginia*, Illustrated by William D. Eubank. undated.

THE ENVIRONS
OF JOHN BROWN'S RAID

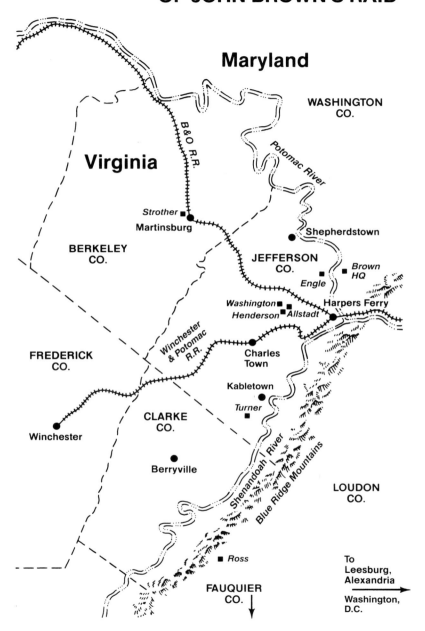

The base map is made from Civil War historian Dennis E. Frye, 2nd Virginia Infantry (1984), with plantation locations, and John Brown's headquarters, added. This Confederate Infantry unit originated in the lower Shenandoah Valley; many were among the Jefferson County militia who contained John Brown at Harpers Ferry.

The locations of the plantations of the slaveholders taken hostage, Washington and Allstadt; Henderson was passed over. David Henderson wrote an account that matches Osborne Anderson's immediately following the raid for his cousin, David Hunter Strother of Martinsburg — "Porte Crayon" of *Harper's Weekly* magazine.

Charles Town, eight miles from Harpers Ferry; the site of John Brown's trial and execution, and burning of barns of the jurors by the local African population

The plantation of George Turner, slaveholder killed in the raid as he came looking for his self-liberated bondsmen. Kabletown is the center of population (the most) fugitives listed on the 1860 census, and of the free community.

Berryville, where an enslaved man was tried for conspiracy and nearly executed in February, 1860 (clemency granted so "impression would not be made that slaves supported Brown.")[4]

Ross plantation in Loudon County, where oral history of the escape of a young slave is documented in the Census of 1860.[5]

Comparison of fugitives to total slave population in Environs counties, Census of 1860

Berkeley County
Total slaves: 1650
Fugitive: 201

Jefferson County
Total slaves: 4014
Fugitive: 612

Loudon County
Total slaves: 5198
Fugitive: 114 (in one location, by Ross)

Clarke County
Total slaves: 3375
Fugitive: 75

Fauquier County (family of Dangerfield Newby)
Total slaves: 10,573
Fugtive: 855

Methodology: The manuscript census Slave Schedules were consulted and calculated from raw data. The reason fugitives were listed was not to pursue them, but to be able to "count" slaves in allocating representatives in Congress — 5 slaves = 3 persons for such allocation. Fugitives listed were usually close to the year of the census taken. This shows a mass movement of self-liberation that John Brown started, but may not have known actually occurred. Not only was the proportion higher in the raid area, the places with slaves gone followed the path of the hostage foray — not at those farms, but smaller ones nearby. The people moved through gaps in the Blue Ridge Mountains, went South near the Ross plantation (where the only fugitives in Loudon County are listed), then toward Leesburg and Alexandria to then escape North. A pattern of family groups are missing in Berkeley and Jefferson counties; mainly single men are gone in Clarke and Fauquier counties.

---

4. Herbert Aptheker, *American Negro Slave Revolts*, (1993), 352-353.

5. Reginald Ross, late of Charles Town and a member of Wainright Baptist Church, said his father escaped at the time of Brown's raid. He returned after the Civil War.

"Shenandoah Street" by Tim Johnson, Falling Waters, West Virginia.
Harpers Ferry was defended by local railroad workers, townspeople, and militia,
who surrounded Brown in the engine house the afternoon of October 17, 1859.
The Shepherdstown Guards wore blue uniforms identical to United States troops
except for the buttons, causing them to be identified as federal forces by Osborne
Anderson in his account written in 1861. See Dennis E. Frye, "Pre–Civil War Militia
of Jefferson County," *Jefferson County Historical Association* (1984).

A Voice From Harper's Ferry

by Osborne P. Anderson, 1861

The method used for excerpting (removing parts of the text) is indicated by . . . . (ellipses). No words have been changed in any of the quoted material. Everything in italics is explanatory from the editor, written in the present day.

The selections begin half way through the original book — Anderson was a participant in the Chatham Convention, and an officer in the Provisional Constitution organization. He is the only person of African descent who signed the Constitution in May, 1858, who came to Harpers Ferry to declare war on slavery with John Brown. He is the only member of Brown's original army who fought in the battles in town on October 17, 1859 and successfully escaped — making "A Voice From Harper's Ferry" the only statement by a participant on John Brown's side who was not in jail in Virginia. The five other members of Brown's army who escaped together were loading arms in Maryland and not part of the battles in town.

Anderson arrived by train at Chambersburg, on September 16, 1859. He walked to the Maryland border on the night of September 24th, was picked up by Brown in a wagon, concealed and brought to the Kennedy farmhouse, where he remained in hiding in the 16×20 foot attic dormitory until Sunday night, October 16, 1859.

The Eleven Orders Given by Captain Brown to His Men Before Setting Out for the Ferry

1. Captain Owen Brown, F.J. Meriam, and Barclay Coppic to remain at the old house as sentinels, to guard the arms and effects until morning, when they would be joined by some of the men from the Ferry with teams to move all arms and other things to the old school-house before referred to, located about three-quarters of a mile from Harper's Ferry.

2. All hands to make as little noise as possible going to the Ferry, so as not to attract attention till we could get to the bridge; and to keep all arms secreted, so as not to be detected if met by anyone.

3. The men were to walk in couples, at some distance apart; and should any one overtake us, stop him and detain him until the rest of our comrades were out of the road. The same course to be pursued if we were met by any one.

27

4. That Captains Charles P. Tidd and John E. Cook walk ahead of the wagon in which Captain Brown rode to the Ferry, to tear down the telegraph wires on the Maryland side along the railroad; and to do the same on the Virginia side, after the town should be captured.

5. Captains John H. Kagi and A.D. Stevens were to take the watchman at the Ferry bridge prisoner when the party got there, and to detain him there until the engine house upon the government grounds should be taken.

6. Captain Watson Brown and Stewart Taylor were to take positions at the Potomac bridge, and hold it till morning. They were to stand on opposite sides, a rod apart, and if any one entered the bridge, they were to let him get in between them. In that case, pikes were to be used, not Sharp's rifles, unless they offered much resistance, and refused to surrender.

7. Captain Oliver Brown and William Thompson were to execute a similar order at the Shenandoah bridge, until morning.

8. Lieutenant Jeremiah Anderson and Aldophus Thomas were to occupy the engine house at first, with the prisoner watchman from the bridge and the watchman belonging to the engine house yard, until the one on the opposite side of the street and the rifle factory were taken, after which they would be reinforced, to hold that place with the prisoners.

9. Lieutenant Albert Hazlett and Private Edwin Coppic were to hold the Armory opposite the engine house after it had been taken, through the night until morning, when arrangements would be different.

10. That John H. Kagi, Adjutant General, and John A. Copeland (colored) take positions at the rifle factory through the night, and hold it until further orders.

11. That Colonel A.D. Stevens . . . proceed to the country with his men, and after taking certain parties prisoners, bring them to the Ferry. In the case of Colonel Lewis Washington, who had arms in his hands, he must, before being secured as a prisoner, deliver them into the hands of Osborne P. Anderson. Anderson being a colored man, and colored men being only *things* in the South, it is proper that the South be taught a lesson upon this point. . . .

The men selected by Col. Stevens to act under his orders during the night were Charles P. Tidd, Osborne P. Anderson, Shields Green, John E. Cook, and Sherrard Lewis Leary. We were to take prisoners, and any slaves who would come, and bring them to the Ferry. . . .

At eight o'clock on Sunday evening, Captain Brown said: "Men, get on your arms. We will proceed to the Ferry." . . . .

The town being taken, Brown, Stevens, and the men who had no post in charge, returned to the engine house, after which Captain Stevens, Tidd, Cook, Shields Green, Leary and myself went to the country. On the road we met some colored men, to whom we make known our purpose, when they immediately agreed to join us. They said they had long been waiting for an opportunity of the kind. Stevens then asked them to go among the colored people and circulate the news, when each started off in a different direction. The result was that many colored men gathered to the scene of the action.

The first prisoner taken by us was Colonel Lewis Washington. When we neared his house, Capt. Stevens placed Leary and Shields Green to guard the approaches to the house, the one at the side, the other in front. We then knocked, but no one answering, although females were looking from upper windows, we entered the building and commenced a search for the proprietor. Col. Washington opened his room door, and begged us not to kill him. Capt. Stevens replied, "You are our prisoner," when he stood as if speechless or petrified. Stevens told him to get ready to go to the Ferry; that he had come to abolish slavery, not to take life but in self-defense, but that he *must* go along. The Colonel replied: "You can have my slaves if you will let me remain. "No," replied the Captain, "you must go along too, now get ready." After saying this, Stevens left the house for a time, and with Green, Leary, and Tidd, proceeded to the "Quarters," giving the prisoner in charge of Cook and myself. The male slaves were gathered together in a short time, when horses were tackled to the Colonel's two-horse carriage and four-horse wagon, and both vehicles brought to the front of the house.

During this time, Washington was walking the floor, apparently much excited. When the Captain came in, he went to the sideboard, took out his whiskey, and offered us something to drink, but he was refused. His fire-arms were next demanded, when he brought forth one double-barrelled gun, one small rifle, two horse-pistols, and a sword. Nothing else was asked of him. . . .

The "guns of October" found in an attic of a black family in Catonsville astonished us with similarity of description to those taken by Osborne P. Anderson at the home of Lewis Washington on the night of October 16, 1859. Those weapons were traced to Civil War service by members of the Woodland family of Maryland, collected for self-defense by veterans of the slave society and to honor John Brown. The origin of one piece in their possession, the small rifle, remains a mystery . . . .

One old colored lady, at whose house we stopped, a little way from the town, had a good time over the message we took her. Liberating the slaves was the very thing she had longed for, prayed for, and dreamed about, time and again; and her heart was full of rejoicing over the fulfilment of a prophecy which had been her faith for long years.

Osborne Anderson now writes of the killing of a B&O Railroad employee, a man of African descent, Haywood (Hayward Shepherd), by Brown's men stationed on the bridges. He was leading an investigating group of railroad employees. Anderson was not a witness to this event. He returned to Harpers Ferry about daylight, the time that medical attention was given to Haywood by Dr. John Starry, several hours after the shooting. Another prisoner, watchman Patrick Higgins — who had been wounded by the same bridge guards — assisted the mortally wounded man in the interim.

While we were absent from the Ferry, the train of cars for Baltimore arrived, and it was detained. A colored man named Haywood, employed upon it, went from the Wager House up to the entrance to the bridge, where the train stood, to assist with the baggage. He was ordered to stop by the sentinels stationed at the bridge, which he refused to do, but turned to go in an opposite direction, when he was fired upon, and received a mortal wound. Had he stood when ordered, he would not have been harmed. No one knew at the time whether he was white or colored, but his movements were such as to justify the sentinels shooting him, as he would not stop when commanded. The first firing happened at that time, and the only firing, until after daylight on Monday morning.

Chapter XI. THE EVENTS OF MONDAY, OCT. 17 — ARMING THE SLAVES — TERROR IN THE SLAVEHOLDING CAMP — IMPORTANT LOSSES TO THE PARTY — THE FATE OF KAGI —PRISONERS ACCUMULATE — WORKMEN AT THE KENNEDY FARM — ETC.

Monday, the 17th of October, was a time of stirring and exciting events. In consequence of the movements of the night before, we were prepared for commotion and tumult, but certainly not for more than we beheld around us. Gray dawn and yet brighter daylight revealed great confusion, and as the sun arose, the panic spread like wild-fire. Men, women, and children could be seen leaving their homes in every direction; some seeking refuge among residents, and in quarters farther away, others climbing up the hill-sides, and hurrying off in various direction, evidently impelled by a sudden fear, which was plainly visible in their countenances or in their movements.

Capt. Brown was all activity, though I could not help thinking that at times he appeared somewhat puzzled. He ordered Sherrard Lewis Leary, and four slaves, and a free man belonging to the neighborhood, to join John Henry Kagi and John Copeland at the rifle factory, which they immediately did. Kagi, and all except Copeland, were subsequently killed, but not before having communicated with Capt. Brown, as will be set forth further along.

As fast as the workmen came to the building, or persons appeared in the street near the engine house, they were taken prisoners, and directly after sunrise, the detained train was permitted to start for the eastward. After the departure of the train, quietness prevailed for a short time; a number of prisoners were already in the engine house, and of the many colored men in the neighborhood, who had assembled in the town, a number were armed for the work.

Capt. Brown ordered Capts. Charles P. Tidd, Wm. H. Leeman, John E. Cook, and some fourteen slaves, to take Washington's four-horse wagon, and to join the company under Capt. Owen Brown, consisting of F.J. Merriam and Barclay Coppic, who had been left at the Farm the night previous, to guard the place and the arms. The company, thus reinforced, proceeded, under Owen Brown, to move the arms and goods from the Farm down to the school-house in the mountains, three fourths of a mile from the Ferry.

Capt. Brown next ordered me to take the pikes out of the wagon in which he rode to the Ferry, and to place them in the hands of the colored men who had come with us from the plantations, and others who had come forward without having had communication with our party. It was out of the circumstances of this order, that the false charge against "Anderson" as leader, or "ringleader" of the negroes, grew. . . .

Anderson next described the second death of a citizen, that of grocer Thomas Boerly, who stepped into the street armed to defend the town. Historians usually credit Dangerfield Newby, one of the black men with Brown who was trying to rescue his wife and children from slavery in Fauquier County, with Boerly's death. Osborne Anderson said it was a local slave.

Anderson's following statement, describing the arrival of troops, has been dismissed as inaccurate by historians. That is because he calls them marines, the Federal troops who do not arrive until Tuesday morning, October 18, under the leadership of United States Army Colonel Robert E. Lee. At noon Monday, when Anderson was still fighting in the arsenal, the Jefferson County militia arrived from across the Potomac River, in military formation. and in blue uniforms, just like Federal soldiers. They drove the raiders into engine house with Brown, killed those who were exposed, and surrounded the engine house. Anderson, leaving the arsenal, then hiding in a basement with Lieut. Albert Hazlett, saw Captain John Brown offer a white flag. He and Hazlett remained hidden until nightfall, then escaped across the Potomac west of Harpers Ferry, near the Engle farm. They were aided by local Africans in these maneuvers. They believed that Brown and their comrades had been captured or killed, and look for their forces on the Maryland side and the liberated slaves. Brown's five men (who also believed that Brown was killed), had left for Pennsylvania. The local Africans did not feel this was a good plan for themselves. They were faced with a survival choice — return to slavery or continue an insurrection which they had not begun.

Among the arms taken from Col. Washington was one double-barrel gun. This weapon was loaded by Leeman with buckshot, and placed in the hands of an elderly slave man, early in the morning. After the cowardly charge upon Coppic, this old man was ordered by Capt. Stevens to arrest a citizen. The old man ordered him to halt, which he refused to do, when instantly the terrible load was discharged into him, and he fell, and expired without a struggle.

After these incidents, time passed away till the arrival of the United States troops, without any further attack upon us. The cowardly Virginians submitted like sheep, without resistance, from that time until the marines came down. Meanwhile, Capt. Brown, who was considering a proposition for release from his prisoners, passed back and forth from the Armory to the bridge, speaking words of comfort and encouragement to his men. "Hold on a little longer, boys," said he, "until I get matters arranged with the prisoners." This tardiness on the part of our brave leader was sensibly felt to be an omen of evil by some of us, and was eventually the cause of our defeat. It was no part of the original plan to hold on to the Ferry, or to parley with the prisoners; but by so doing, time was afforded to carry the news of its capture to several points, and forces were thrown into place, which surrounded us.

CHAPTER XII. RECEPTION TO THE TROOPS — THEY RETREAT TO THE BRIDGE — A PRISONER — DEATH OF DANGERFIELD NEWBY — WILLIAM THOMPSON — THE MOUNTAINS ALIVE — FLAG OF TRUCE —THE ENGINE HOUSE TAKEN

It was about twelve o'clock in the day when we were first attacked by the troops. Prior to that, in anticipation of further trouble, Capt. Brown had girded to his side the famous sword taken from Col. Lewis Washington the night before, and with that memorable weapon, he commanded his men against General Washington's own State.

When the Captain received the news that the troops had entered the bridge from the Maryland side, he, with some of his men, went into the street, and sent a message to the Arsenal for us to come forth also. We hastened to the street as ordered, when he said — "The troops are on the bridge, coming into town; we will give them a warm reception. He then walked around amongst us, giving us words of encouragement, in this wise: "Men, be cool! Take aim, and make every last shot count." "The troops will look to us to retreat at their first appearance, be careful to shoot first." Our men were well supplied with firearms, but Capt. Brown had no rifle at that time; his only weapon was the sword before mentioned. . . .

On the retreat of the troops, we were ordered back to our former post. While going, Dangerfield Newby, one of our colored men, was shot through the head by a person who took aim at him from a brick store window, on the opposite side of the street, and who was there for the purpose of firing upon us. Newby was a brave fellow.

He was one of my comrades at the Arsenal. He fell at my side, and his death was promptly avenged by Shields Green, the Zouave of the band, who afterwards met his fate calmly on the gallows, with John Copeland. Newby was shot twice; at the first fire, he fell on his side and returned it; as he lay, a second shot was fired, and the ball entered his head. Green raised his rifle in an instant, and brought down the cowardly murderer, before the latter could get his gun back through the sash. . . .

Osborne Anderson believed that many more Virginians were killed than in published totals, basing his own perception from the middle of the battle, and his later justification of saving his own life, leaving the fray in the midafternoon with his officer in charge, Albert Hazlett, who was captured in Pennsylvania after the two separated. Although Brown pretended he did not know Hazlett in prison, he was tried, convicted, and executed with Aaron Stevens on March 16, 1860.

When John Brown was captured on the morning of October 18, Jerry Anderson was killed in the engine house by a marine with a bayonet. He was identified as a mulatto (which was Osborne Anderson's description) by the severely wounded Stevens, under interrogation by the Virginians at the hotel. Jeremiah Anderson was then mutilated and stuffed into a barrel, and taken to the medical school in Winchester — also the fate of the two black army members who were hanged, Shields Green and John Copeland.

All this time, the fight was progressing; no powder and ball were wasted. We shot from under cover, and took deadly aim. For an hour before the flag of truce was sent out, the firing was uninterrupted, and one and another of the enemy were constantly dropping to the earth.

One of the Captain's plans was to keep up communication between his three points. In carrying out this idea, Jerry Anderson went to the rifle factory, to see Kagi and his men. Kagi, fearing that we would be overpowered by numbers if the Captain delayed leaving, sent word by Anderson to advise him to leave the town at once. This word Anderson communicated to the Captain, and told us also at the Arsenal. The message sent back to Kagi was, to hold out for a few minutes longer, when we would all evacuate the place. Those few minutes proved disastrous, for it was then that the troops before spoken of came pouring in, increased by crowds of men from the surrounding country. After an hour's hard fighting, and when the enemy were blocking up the avenues of escape, Capt. Brown sent out his son Watson with a flag of truce, but no respect was paid to it; he was fired upon, and wounded severely. He returned to the engine house, and fought bravely after that for fully a day and a half, when he received a mortal wound, which he struggled under until the next day. . . .

Capt. A.D. Stevens was next sent out with a flag, with what success I will presently show. Meantime, Jeremiah Anderson, who had brought the message from Kagi previously, was sent by Capt. Brown with another message to John Henrie, but before he got far on the street, he was fired upon and wounded. He returned at once to the engine house, where he survived but a short time. The ball, it was found, had entered the right side in such manner that death necessarily ensued rapidly.

After the capture of Stevens, desperate fighting was done by both sides. The marines forced their way into the engine-house yard. and commanded Capt. Brown to surrender, but refused to do, but said in reply, that he was willing to fight them, if they would allow him first to withdraw his men to the second lock on the Maryland side. As might be expected, the cowardly hordes refused to entertain such a proposition, but continued their assault, to cut off communication between our several parties. . . .

Anderson and Hazlett left the scene of the fighting, hiding for some time in a basement. After dark (they had been awake and under the stress of the event for at least thirty-six hours) they made their way to the Potomac behind the town, claiming they took a townsman hostage, found a rowboat, and crossed the river. Had he written of assistance by local people in 1861, they would be endangered. No white townsman has ever come forward.

What Anderson and Hazlett actually saw were Frederick, Maryland militia arrive by train at dusk, surround John Brown's fort, and parley with him under a white flag. They began to fight anew, but then did not storm the engine house for fear of harming the hostage slaveholders. Anderson and Hazlett were then fleeing for their lives. They heard the firing of Brown's actual capture across the Potomac on Tuesday morning, after finding their five companions loading arms gone, and all weapons and materials taken from the farmhouse by the Maryland militia the previous night. They met some of the local men who had joined them the day before, firing across the Potomac River, and told them of the failure of their enterprise and the capture of John Brown.

Maryland Heights and covered B&O R.R. Bridge, ca. 1859 (continued at right)

It was after sunrise some time when we awoke in the morning. The first sound we heard was shooting at the Ferry. Hazlett thought it must be Owen Brown and his men trying to force their way into the town, as they had been informed a number of us were taken prisoners, and we started down along the ridge to join them. When we got in sight of the Ferry, we saw the troops firing across the river to the Maryland side with considerable spirit. Looking closely, we saw, to our surprise, that they were firing upon a few of the colored men, who had been armed the day before by our men, at the Kennedy Farm, and stationed down at the schoolhouse by C.P. Tidd. They were in the bushes on the edge of the mountains, dodging about, occasionally exposing themselves to the enemy. The troops crossed the bridge in pursuit of them, but they retreated in

Osborne P. Anderson
1829-1872
(Courtesy Kansas State
Historical Society)

different directions. Being further in the mountains, and more secure, we could see without personal harm befalling us. One of the colored men came towards where we were, when we hailed him, and inquired the particulars. He said that one of his comrades had been shot, and was lying on the side of the mountains; that they thought the men who had armed them the day before must be in the Ferry. That opinion, we told him, was not correct. We asked him to join with us in hunting up the rest of the party, but he declined, and went his way.

Maryland Heights and covered B&O R.R. Bridge, ca. 1859 (National Park Service)

TWO TRAINS

ONE OF THE major mysteries of John Brown histories is the selective elimination of primary sources when Africans were at the center of the action. The most serious of these omissions is the absence of a second train, a mail express, which was stopped in Maryland, near the Harpers Ferry bridge, by armed black men. The passenger train going east, stopped at Harpers Ferry in the midnight hours, is well-known. John Brown allowed the passenger train to proceed toward Baltimore by 3:00 a.m., but the engineer did not want to do so until daylight. He was fearful of the numbers of men guarding the track, . . . telling the panicked passengers inside that they "longed for liberty."

From the Harpers Ferry bridge to Point of Rocks, three miles east, there was a single track. There was a switch near the bridge, which is where the second train, the mail train from Baltimore, was stopped "on the Maryland side . . . by an insurrection in progress in which free negroes and whites are engaged."

SHEPHERDSTOWN REGISTER.

$2 per annum, to be paid before the year expires.   JOHN H. ZITTLE, EDITOR AND PROPRIETOR. $2 per annum, to be paid before the year expires.

A Family Newspaper--Devoted to General Intelligence, Advertising, Literature, Morality, Agriculture, Arts and Sciences, Markets, &c., &c.

VOL. VIII.   SHEPHERDSTOWN, JEFFERSON COUNTY, VA., SATURDAY MORNING, OCTOBER 22, 1859.   NO.

Slave Insurrection at
HARPER'S FERRY.

GREAT EXCITEMENT!

The Armory seized and trains stopped!

CARS FIRED INTO !

VIRGINIA AND MARYLAND
MILITARY ORDERED OUT !

*CITIZEN'S TAKEN
PRISONERS*

Blood Shed and Lives Lost !

The Insurrectionists Routed !

Part of them flee to the
Mountain !

PURSUIT !

The Commander-in-Chief and
the Insurrectionists Captured,
&c., &c.

The following dispatches were sent to the Baltimore Clipper from Frederick city, Md., (the telegraph wires at Harper's Ferry being cut east and west) at 2 o'clock, Monday morning [Oct. 17, 1859].

Frederick, Oct. 17. — Information has been received here this morning of a formidable negro insurrection in Harper's Ferry and the United States Arsenal. The express train was fired into twice, and one of the hands, a negro, was killed whilst trying to get the train through the town.

They have arrested two men who came with a load of wheat and took their wagon and loaded it with rifles, and sent them into Maryland. They are led by about fifty whites with a gang of negroes fighting for their freedom. They gave Conductor Phelps notice that they would not allow any more trains to pass.

Statement of Conductor Phelps and his Officers.

In the meantime, other persons from the train ventured across the bridge above the Ferry, and soon coming into contact with the rioters (who were reputed at almost two hundred in number, half of whom seemed to be black,) one of the party, a passenger, was captured. The train was detained by the proceedings until half-past six o'clock, when steam was raised, and they reached the Camden station at noon to-day. . . .

The engineer states that amongst them there were several strapping negroes who occasionally shouted that they longed for liberty, as they had been in bondage long enough. . . .

The officers report that the United States Armory and the neighboring country have been taken possession of by the rioters, all of whom are well armed with short rifles and other United States arms. When the workmen of the armory repaired there for the purpose of resuming work they were seized by the parties, forcibly dragged within the gates and imprisoned.

Harpers Ferry, from *Johnson's New Illustrated Family Atlas of the World,* A.J. Johnson, 1865

Dispatches from the new and active President of the B&O Railroad, John W. Garrett, the passenger train conductor, Phelps, and John Quyunn, agent in Frederick, tell the story of John Brown's raid in the early hours. It was the B&O Railroad bridge that was captured, railroad employees made prisoner, wounded, and killed (a conductor during the fighting, as well as Haywood). Trains would be needed to bring troops from Baltimore and Washington, D.C.

In his dispatches, John Garrett frequently mentioned black men in arms. In the following telegraph, sent at 4:38 p.m. on October 17, 1859, Garrett told the President of the United States that it was both free blacks and slaves who were in John Brown's army.

James Buchanan, President of the United States, Washington:

All the trains on the road are stopped. The mail train going West has been stopped and forced to return, and the conductor made prisoner. Our agents report by telegraphs that seven hundred whites and blacks are in arms and in full possession of the U.S. Armory. They report also that the slaves are taken possession of by the insurrectionists. It is a moment full of peril. General Steuart is awaiting your reply.

John W. Garrett
President of the B&O Railroad

This telegram was sent by the B&O Railroad agent in Frederick, John T. Quynn, to the newspapers in Baltimore in midday of October 17. He did so because he was getting a stalling action from his supervisor, W. P. Smith, the Master of Transportation in Baltimore, not to send the Maryland militia who had gathered in Frederick, "unless upon the formal requisition of an authorized officer at Harper's Ferry." Quyunn knew the town to be in the control of John Brown, as well as telegraph communication cut.

To the Baltimore Newspaper Press

Information has been received here this morning of a formidable negro insurrection at Harper's Ferry. An armed band of abolitionists have full possession of Harper's Ferry and the United States Arsenal. One of the railroad hands, a negro, was killed whilst trying to get the express train, from Wheeling to Baltimore, through the town.

They have arrested two men who came in with a load of wheat, and took their wagon and loaded it with rifles, and sent them into Maryland. They are led by about two hundred and fifty whites, with a gang of negroes fighting for their freedom. They gave conductor Phelps notice that they would not allow any more trains to pass. The telegraph wires are cut east and west of Harper's Ferry. This intelligence was brought by the train from the West. Great excitement here. The leader told Conductor Phelps, of the Baltimore and Ohio Railroad train, that they *were determined to have liberty, or die in the attempt.*" [italics in original]

The railroad president — who would become one of Lincoln's most able associates in winning the Civil War with "hands on" train management — notified the Maryland militia in time for three companies to be organized in Frederick by 10 a.m., following the first telegram from Conductor Phelps of the eastbound passenger train at 7:05 a.m.

However, the commander decided to go by train himself to Gibson's Switch, at the bridge, before bringing the 16th Regiment, and from his reconnaissance asked for a cannon to accompany the men, delaying their entry in Harpers Ferry until dusk. The only consistent information that was available, according to Col. Shriver's rediscovered report in the Maryland State Archives, was that "several hunded whites and blacks were engaged in the insurrection."

Who were the black men who stopped the second train? All the original five men of Africa in Brown's group were in Virginia. They were specifically, and at the moment (afternoon of October 17), identified as free by John W. Garrett to the President of the United States. How did he know they weren't the slaves sent over by wagon in the early morning to load arms?

Understanding the free African community of Maryland is essential. This was an area that had many free persons of color, skilled ironworkers and workers on the B&O Railroad itself. They lived throughout the valleys, in and near Frederick. Their ancestors had been ironworkers, and established independent churches. One of these early groups is now Mt. Moriah Baptist Church in Garrett's Mill.

Black workers on the B&O Railroad at Gibson's Switch were specifically free. This was a policy created by a previous president of the B&O, Caspar Wever, who placed freed workers on his farm, called Weverton, and also funded settlement in Liberia through the Maryland Colonization Society, which began in 1831 for manumitted Africans.

At the time of Brown's raid, many workers lived in the community of Knoxville, where a track went from Frederick down the mountain to meet the track alongside the Potomac River. The still-active Mt. Zion A.M.E. church, founded by Thomas W. Henry in the 1840s, drew congregants "from Harper's Ferry, and a great many from a considerable distance in Virginia," where it was illegal for free African ministers to preach.

Thomas Henry, born and enslaved in 1794, provides an unparalleled source of the social history of the Africans who lived in Washington and Frederick counties in the 1840s and 1850s. As a blacksmith, he was aware of the technology that was used in ironmaking in these hills and valleys, which was predominantly enslaved workers, often African-born, in the iron industry in Maryland. As in African tradition, where blacksmiths are mediators, the Rev. Thomas W. Henry, who became part of the African Methodist Episcopal Church in 1835, was in the mediator tradition of ministers that continues to this day.

He wrote of an insurrection of ironworkers at the Antietam Works that occurred about fifteen years before John Brown arrived in the neighborhood to organize his army. This incident — which he helped to mediate — involved the attempted whipping of enslaved workers by the white manager and European — often European-born — workers. The movement among these white workers was an attempt to establish hegemony over skilled occupations, which were frequently performed by skilled Africans building on the technology that was in their homeland. Forges, especially, reflected these African influences in the southern iron industry. These techniques were changing to the use of puddling, a European method, which produced more quantities of iron of a lesser quality. The Antietam Ironworks was a regular supplier of the Harpers Ferry armory across the Potomac River, although in 1859 the rebellious slave community was gone, the victims of depressed conditions in the previous decade, sold to pay the insolvent owner's debts.

Early ironmasters McPherson and Brien, like Caspar Wever, sent freed persons to Liberia. Likewise, the Rev. Thomas W. Henry was an agent of the American Colonization Society in 1827, which sent persons in his ministerial circuits to African shores to build a new society based upon Christian mission. Like the later Maryland Colonization Society, ACS was formed by slaveholders.

John Brown entered these hills and valleys in the summer of 1859. Commenting on how useful the mountains would be to establish a protective area for liberating the enslaved, he sought local free persons of African descent. In July, 1859, he wrote to John Kagi:

> Get Mr. Watson to find out, if he can, a trusty man, or men, to stop with at Hagerstown (if any such there be), as Mr. Thomas Henrie has gone from there.

This letter appeared on the front page of the Baltimore Sun on November 10, 1859. The elder minister considered it natural that "that good old saint" *John Brown would have* "a memorandum for him to find me with" *but was persuaded by friends in Baltimore (also A.M.E. ministers) that he should leave before being arrested. He did so with their assistance, and with that of a white man who was also a member of the Masonic order —* "for he knew I was the widow' son." *His Autobiography was written in 1872. It is the only written account of the raid by a local person of African descent living at the time of the action:* "Look, for instance, at the fertile hills of Charlestown, W. Va., literally stained with blood."

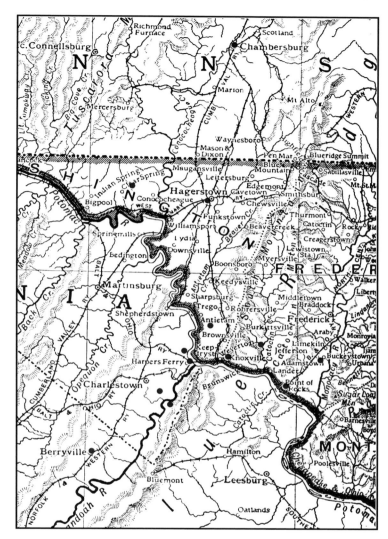

• locations of African support for
John Brown's war on slavery, 1859

1 inch = 16 miles

Base map: *Encyclopedia Britannica,* 1911

ALLIES FOR FREEDOM

General Moses (Harriet Tubman)
by Charles White, 1965

Virginian African wagoner
by Porte Crayon, 1857

I am succeding to all appearances beyond my expectations. Harriet Tubman hooked on his whole team at once. He, Harriet, is the most of a man naturally; that I ever met with. There is the most abundant material; & of the right quality: in this quarter, beyond all doubt. Do not forget to write Mr. Case (near Rochester) at once about hunting every person & family of the reliable kind; about, of, or near Bedford, Chambersburg, Gettysburg, & Carlisle in Pa., & also Hagerstown & vicinity maryland; & Harper's Ferry, Va.

John Brown to John Brown, Jr.
Chatham, Canada West
April, 1858

Benjamin A. Matthews wrote a history of the John Brown raid for the Storer Sentinal *on the 50th anniversary. He included information about local people getting weapons that is not seen in any other history of the event. He was a member of the Mt. Moriah Baptist Church, which was*  *founded by the same missionaries who established Storer College for freedmen and Indians just after the Civil War. Visiting the church in 1979, the editor met his sister-in-law, Mrs. Pearl Matthews. She remembered him well. Benjamin and her husband, Daniel Matthews, served in the United States armed forces in World War I. Mrs. Matthews and Mrs. Marie Claybon, the wife of the minister, also remembered an earlier minister of their church, Rev. John Newman, telling them as children to "always remember." John Brown s war on slavery that took place in these hills, an area known as South Mountain. This was the Underground Railroad route from the Shenandoah Valley to Chambersburg, Pennsylvania.*

Harper's Ferry and John Brown

The neighboring mountains, with their inaccessible fastnesses with which John Brown had been familiar for seventeen years, afforded a thousand opportunities. He was an abolitionist and believed that slavery should be stamped out by the quickest possible means. It was the original intention of Captain Brown to seize the arsenal at Harper's Ferry on the night of October 24, 1859, and to take the arms there deposited to add to his ammunition in the neighboring mountains. . . .

Brown's plan was for the negroes to march with such arms as they could lay their hands on, and as soon as possible reach the free states of the North. Nevertheless he expected them to use whatever force might be necessary to accomplish that end. He provided the majority with guns, pistols, and spears.

In Harm's Way:
African Americans in Jefferson County, Virginia, 1859

Verse 1:
Living below in this old sinful world
Hardly a comfort can afford.
Striving alone to face temptation's
"shore,"
Where could I go but to the Lord?

Chorus:
Where could I go — oh, where could I go
Seeking a refuge for my soul?
Needing a friend to save me in the end —
Where could I go but to the Lord?[1]

ONE OF THE few things that distinguished the enslaved from those of free- and freed-status in the Civil War era was that of being a property owner, with ease of movement in varying degrees.[2] For Jefferson County's African American population, ownership of land often-times came out of great personal sacrifice and, together with one's freedom, was counted among life's most profound blessings and prized possessions. Yet these same citizens, as a result of the War between the States spilling over within close proximity to their houses and farms, were being driven from their home-places. For some, it must have been a most perplexing, disheartening enigma — whereas the Union Army's mission in freeing the slaves would change the destiny of African Americans for all time, it would simultaneously cost many free men and women all for which they had sacrificed: their homes, their families, and sense of well-being as long as the conflict lasted.

---

1. "Where Could I Go But to the Lord?" is an old Negro spiritual, probably written around 1900, according to Rev. Walter A. Jackson, Pastor of Wainwright Baptist Church in Charles Town (May 28, 1999). Other than memory banks, the sole location for such musical numbers would have been the old "words-only" paperback songbooks passed down from generation to generation by the faithful. Its message, a symbolic longing for spiritual refuge, also has an earthly counterpart: inasmuch as slaves longed for their freedom, free men and women also sought solace and peace in their homeplaces that were being ravaged by war.

2. In his research, James L. Taylor, former educator in Jefferson County public schools, member of the Charles Town Historic Landmarks Commission, and current researcher on local African American history, has divided African Americans residing in the county during the 1850-60s into five basic categories: (1) free blacks who were never enslaved (e.g., Martin Delany); (2) freed blacks who were former slaves; (3) enslaved blacks; (4) slaves living as free (i.e., could work, earn a wage, save their money, and purchase their freedom); and (5) freed blacks living as slaves (e.g., Haywood Shepherd who attached himself to Harpers Ferry's mayor, Fontaine Beckham). Interview conducted with Mr. Taylor on May 27, 1999.

No less, the immediate decision to join or wait — plus the surprise element of Brown's 1859 raid on the Federal arsenal at Harpers Ferry — put both free and enslaved persons in Jefferson County in harm's way when the greatly outnumbering whites effectively contained, then captured, John Brown and his small forces. This paper documents and describes free African communities in the county in 1859, and connects the free and enslaved through their common worship in congregations which were forming before the Civil War. These emerged as independent churches among the emancipated generation soon thereafter.

Most of the free Africans lived in Kabletown, Rippon, Shannondale, and Bolivar. Jackson Newman, a "free man of color" who had purchased a 10-acre tract of river-front property on the east side of the Shenandoah River in the Blue Ridge on February 23, 1859 from Mary Ann Myers.[3] Two large Newman families, headed by Jackson Newman and George Newman, lived in proximity in 1860. They were farm laborers, as well as individual single men living at white farms. The free families of African descent in the county lived near each other wherever they were present – their numbers were small – 473 persons in a total of 10,317 whites and 4014 slaves.[4]

Other pioneer free families seen in the 1860 census were Goins (census spelling, also Goens), Freeman, Johnson, Roper, and Harris. Thomas Goins, 34, and Lawson Goins, 53, were blacksmiths with their own businesses, while younger men, such as William Johnson, 21, were blacksmiths in white establishments, not apprentices. Anthony Welcome, 53, was among the thirty-nine free blacks (mainly children) living in town in Harpers Ferry. He maintained his own blacksmith business. Harpers Ferry

---

3. Jackson Newman property deed, Jefferson County Courthouse, Deed Book 39, p. 126. Evelyn M.E. Taylor, ed., *Final Report on the 1992 Brookins/Howell-Hall-Tolbert-Newman Family Reunion*, Jefferson County, West Va., October 30, 1992, sections of which were published, "County Family Meets, Past History Recalled at Event," *Spirit of Jefferson Farmer's Advocate*, November 19, 1992.

4. In 1977 and 1978, Jean Libby, for *Black Voices From Harpers Ferry* (Berkeley, Calif., 1979), interviewed people descended from many generations who had lived in the county: The late Mrs. Effie Dennis Allen and the late Miss Charlotte Lovett of Harpers Ferry, the late Prof. John Wesley Harris of Shepherdstown, and Mr. and Mrs. Russell Roper of Charles Town. In Maryland: The late Mrs. Pearl Matthews, the late Mrs. Marie Claybon, and Mrs. Marguerite Doleman, historian. These interviews suggested support for John Brown by the Newman family through a Baptist minister, Rev. John Newman, or a Baptist Sunday school teacher, Brother Albert Newman. Jackson Newman's acreage on the Shenandoah River, purchased in 1859, could have been used to provide passage to fugitives, as graphed on page 25 of this volume. It is hard to imagine the enormous risk to his livelihood such activity would entail at the time of John Brown's raid.

boatman Joseph Blanham was imprisoned in the 1840s for helping fugitives but returned to his occupation after release.[5]

Free families who lived within close proximity knew each other and, despite the War between the States that began with John Brown's armed incursion, attempted to live normal lives. Farming was a way of life for most county residents, black or white. Others living within a few miles of the Jackson Newmans near Shannondale were B.F. Howell and his family.[6]

Both the Howell and Newman families cultivated their properties. Various fruit trees and flowering shrubs, and vegetable gardens peppered the acreage. A favorite past time among the younger siblings was climbing the trees. Edward Howell entered a skilled trade as a cooper or cabinet-maker, traveling by train to jobs as far away as Chambersburg, Pennsylvania, seventy miles from Charles Town.[7] Siblings grew up, took spouses and started families, often living within a short distance from their parents and other family members. Because of the law requiring manumitted slaves to leave the state within the year, the free population grew before the Civil War by marrying within the group, creating a core society that is intertwined to the present day.

---

5. The census records of 1850 and 1860 were read by Jean Libby for this publication. African Americans, such as Joseph Blanham, who lived in lower town Harpers Ferry in both censuses are mapped in a permanent exhibition, "Black Voices From Harpers Ferry," by Charles Snell, Melinda Day, David Larson, John King, Gwen Roper, and Marsha Starkey, the research team at Harpers Ferry National Historic Monument, building on work begun by historian Paul Lee of the National Park Service.

6. Record of Wills, Book 80, p. 8. Edward Howell was the paternal great grandfather of this author and the maternal grandfather of Mrs. Florence Newman Brown. In an April 3, 1999 interview with Edward Howell's 90-year-old grandson, Thomas Newman, a resident of Baltimore, Md., it is surmised that B.F. Howell, the probable father of Edward Howell (b. 1852; d. April 16, 1906), bestowed a gift of land in 1895 to the Howell couple just as any father would do on behalf of his son. The conveyance to the couple was "for and during their natural life and at their death to the children . . . their heirs and assigns forever." Whereas Jackson Newman's property was sold decades ago, the Howell property has remained in family hands. It survived Edward's controversial death in the Jefferson County jail on April 16, 1906. See "Killed Over a Spring," *Farmer's Advocate*, January 16, 1906 and April 24, 1906. See also Hannah Geffert, "Ed Howell's Spring Incident," *An Annotated Narrative of the African-American Community in Jefferson County, West Virginia*, Jefferson County and Berkeley County branches of the NAACP, July 15, 1992, p. 104. Whereas the white community has held to the fabrication that Edward Howell committed suicide by hanging himself while incarcerated, numerous voices — black and white, family and nonfamily — concur that Howell's death occurred as a result of being lynched while imprisoned. Lynching was often the price a black paid for killing a white in 1906. Further, Professor Geffert's interview indicates that Edward Howell remained a resident of the Shannondale area of Jefferson County from the time of his birth.

Other free families, such as the Ropers who lived south and east of Charles Town, occupied two large adjacent farms: Pleasant View, 334 acres; and Cattail, 277 acres. These properties under Roper ownership can be traced to November 28, 1822, in a large purchase made by James Roper from Roger Humphrey.[8]

Some of the Ropers were eye-witnesses of local Civil War activity. They were William Roper and wife, Sally Goens Roper, grandparents of current Jefferson County resident, Russell Roper. In a 1929-30 account shared with grandson Russell Roper, Sally Roper spoke of the experiences she had with soldiers while she and husband William maintained a small tobacco farm near Clipp's Mill on the Kabletown Road in close proximity to the Shenandoah River. She personally sold tobacco to both Union and Confederate soldiers.

A few points of demography about the area: In racial make-up, contemporary Shannondale, east of the Shenandoah River, has a minuscule number of African Americans, whereas far more black settlers lived there during the Civil War. Kabletown, on the west side of the Shenandoah, had a burgeoning number of African Americans that continued well past the turn of the century. Currently, only a small fraction of the county's black population lives in the Kabletown-Myerstown area.

This essay opened with the old Negro spiritual, "Where Could I Go But to the Lord?" whose inspiration no doubt came from life's experiences and recollections, reaching back into the pre-Civil War period. Regardless, life's comforts were few; and, one could not always rely on friends. Out of that experience came the piercing spirituals, hymns and slave songs indicative of their faith and reliance on God. It was no different for African Americans in Jefferson County. Black people sought solace and peace from the Supreme Being. The Almighty was the source of their hope, the focus of their pleas, and the one from whom they sought answers to life's most complex

---

7. A "pie-safe" to house freshly-baked pies, built by Edward Howell sometime before his untimely death, is a testament to this free man of color whose skill in wood-carving and cabinet-making was legendary. The oak safe with carved doors contructed without nails and pins, has been preserved and passed down in the family. It is currently in the hands of Jefferson County educator, Ms. Carolyn Bradford, great-great grand-daughter of Edward. Pie-safes have recently been reintroduced to American homes.

8. Deedbook, 129, p. 94; property also featured on 1883 Jefferson County Courthouse map; interview with Russell Roper, Jefferson County contractor and builder, May 27, 1999. According to Mr. Roper, the earliest known Roper ethnicity connection originates in Ireland when Ropers immigrated to the United States and settled in Jefferson County. It is not known when members split into Euro-American and Afro-American segments. White Ropers and black Ropers both acknowledge their membership in the same family.

problems. Records of their public worship do not appear until the second half of the 1800s; however, indications of religious activity among blacks relate back to the 1700s.

An 1832 Virginia state law following the insurrection of Nat Turner in 1831 silenced all black preachers. (Of course, there were exceptions where slaves met for worship secretly, often by cover of night, with black ministers who risked all that they had to experience fellowship among their kinsman.) Churches had hitherto flourished in eastern Virginia in the first quarter of the century, but freedom of worship was to be completely halted. Under Governor Floyd, the Virginia legislature decreed, "no slave, free Negro or mulatto shall preach, or hold any meeting for religious purposes either day or night . . . religious instruction may be given in the day time by a licensed white minister."[9]

The earliest organized churches serving the white population were founded throughout Jefferson County as early as the 1740s.[10] Many of these churches provided segregated quarters for the black congregants, out of which led to the founding of some of the local black congregations, such as St. Philip's Episcopal Church in the heart of Charles Town's African American community today.

Documentation reveals the existence of a slave congregation in Shepherdstown, St. Andrew's Episcopal Church (Colored), presided over by the Rev. Charles W. Andrews, Rector of Trinity Episcopal Church. The black church was founded in 1859, according to Trinity Church's minute books that recorded slave births, confirmations, communicants, weddings, and funerals during the period 1843-1896. Because slaves were obligated to prepare and serve slaveholders' Sunday dinner, among other duties, they could not always attend worship with their owners, who were among Trinity Episcopal Church's white congregants. For many, their respite came later in the day. The slaves' desire to meet for worship on Sunday evenings met with approval, and Rev. Andrews agreed to be their minister. These same slaves held such high regard for the rector that they named their church after him. Trinity Episcopal arranged for the slaves to use their old building when the new edifice was erected between 1855-59; it was consecrated for use in 1859. Trinity was also the holder of the St. Andrew's deed

9. Virginia Writers' Project, *The Negro in Virginia.* Winston-Salem, N.C.: John F. Blair, Publishers, 1994 (originally published New York: Hastings House, 1940).

10. South Jefferson Ministerial Association, *Charles Town Bicentennial, 1786-1986, Ecumenical Worship Service* Program Brochure.

could not own property. The minutes also describe aspects of life among black slaves — fugitives were listed as well as those whose faithful attendance had somehow slipped. The only mentioning of free people occurred, for example, when a marriage united an Episcopalian slave and a free person.[11] This congregation became African Methodist Eopsicopal in 1864; it is now United Methodist. They moved from the old Episcopal building in the 1980s; it is still extant.

Before the founding of St. Philip's Episcopal Chapel (Colored) in 1867 in Charles Town, Zion Episcopal Church, which was organized in 1815, reserved its gallery for black congregants. Records do not distinguish between enslaved and free. Zion Church recorded baptisms of 20 black infants as early as 1838, confirmed three persons of color in 1847, and reported 10 "colored" Sunday School teachers and 50 students in 1858.[12]

There is no doubt local black churches included worshippers who were enslaved, as well as free blacks, during the John Brown era. However, little is known about them in the absence of records. Some helped with the building of these churches. For example, those who built Zion Baptist Church in Charles Town were former slaves who had previously worshipped at First Baptist Church, also in Charles Town. Other black congregations that sprang up mostly, but not exclusively, during the latter half of the 1800s include the following:

- Mt. Zion Free Will Baptist Church, Johnsontown (organized as Johnsontown Community Church ca.1848; established in 1898 as Mt. Zion Free Will Baptist)
- Asbury United Methodist, Shepherdstown (founded originally as St. Andrew's Episcopal in 1859 but evolved as a Methodist congregation in 1864)
- Mt. Zion United Methodist Church, Charles Town (ca.1866)
- St. Philip's Episcopal Church (1867 as mentioned above)
- Curtis Memorial Chapel - Storer College, Harpers Ferry (1867)
- St. John Baptist Church, Shepherdstown (1868)
- Wainwright Baptist Church, Charles Town (1868)

11. Evelyn ME. Taylor, *Historical Digest of Jefferson County, West Virginia's African American Congregations, 1859-1994 (with selected churches in neighboring Berkeley County, W.Va., Maryland and Virginia)*, Washington, D.C.: Middle Atlantic Regional Press, 1999, pp. 133-41.

12. George W. Peterkin, *A History and Record of the Protestant Episcopal Church in Diocese of West Virginia and, Before the Formation of the Diocese in 1878, in the Territory Now Known as the State of West Virginia*, 1902.

- John Wesley United Methodist Church, Harpers Ferry (1869)
- A circuit of three African Methodist Episcopal congregations:
  Mt. Zion A.M.E., Duffields (1870);
  Mt. Zion A.M.E., Mt. Pleasant (1870)
  Stewart Chapel A.M.E., Kearneysville (1890)
- Ebenezer Methodist Church in Mt. Pleasant (1879)
- St. Paul's Baptist Church, Kearneysville (1879)
- Zion Baptist Church, Charles Town (1881)
- First Zion Baptist Church, Harpers Ferry (1893)
- Second Zion Primitive Baptist Church, Rippon (also called Old School Baptist, ca. late 1800s)

Wainwright, St. John, and Curtis Memorial Baptist churches were among the several churches founded in the 1860s by five missionaries from New England: Dr. Nathan C. Brackett, Mrs. Louise Brackett, Mrs. Laura Brackett, Rev. Alexander H. Morrell, and Miss Annie Dudley.[13] Their sponsor was the Shenandoah Valley Yearly Meeting, later known as the Brackett-Morrell Association. Resulting from their labors were twelve African American congregations, including Dudley Baptist Church in Martinsburg, founded in 1867, and several others in Berryville, Winchester, Staunton, and Luray, Virginia.[14]

Although not officially established until 1898, a Baptist congregation founded in Jefferson County by the Johnson family was organized in 1848, the same year the community of Johnsontown was established, considered to be one of Jefferson County's safe-havens for escaping slaves.[15] George W. Johnson was the founder of Johnsontown, the first and only known community in the county named after an African American.[16] Johnsontown emerged as a safe, connected village of farmers with the Johnsontown Community Church, Free-Will Baptist in theology, at its center. Its free-will

---

13. "The Brackett-Morrell Baptist Association," in *Centennial Anniversary of Mt. Moriah Baptist Church, 1890-1990,* May 20-26, 1990, p. 6. In addition to the founding of churches, schools, including Storer College, were established by these missionaries.

14. Taylor, *Historical Digest,* ch. 28.

15. Stephen Willingham, "From Bondage to Freedom: A Talk with Jerry Johnson," *Good News Paper* Shepherdstown, W.Va. Ministerial Association's twentieth anniversary edition, Summer 1999, p. 6 (originally appeared in Spring 1996 edition).

16. Jerry Myers Johnson, "Johnsontown, West Virginia Heritage Yearbook, 1987," vol. I, no. 1, and "The New Covenant, Johnsontown Heritage History Book," undated. Hannah Geffert, *An Annotated Narrative of African-American History in Jefferson County,* 1992.

heritage came from its early pioneer connections with the "Church German Abolitionists," immigrants who had settled in Pennsylania between 1684 and 1835.[17]

The foregoing narrative outlines records of public worship by both enslaved and free African Americans in Jefferson County in the 1850-1860s. Whether examining their worship in segregated galleries in white churches or centers of religious worship in their own meeting houses and edifices, area blacks had a religious heritage whose teachings did not all originate with local white slaveholders.

There is, moreover, earlier documented evidence of theological teachings and aspects of religious worship that was introduced to the area as early as 1751, the period known as the Great Awakening. New Light Baptists from Connecticut arrived in Virginia bringing with them a fundamentalist perspective on the preaching of the Gospel: Anyone could be called to preach the Gospel and become His messengers. Such a calling was not a self-appointment or the result of attending seminary, training that only a select few could afford. New Light Baptists believed this Pentecostal calling crossed racial and socioeconomic lines, so that African people, enslaved and free, Native Americans, and poor whites were just as eligible to become God's voice as those whose circumstances produced the most visible leadership roles in Protestant churches.[18]

Many a camp-meeting and covert backwoods gathering of Afro-Virginians for worship were presided over by ministers who lacked the formal credentials of seminary but whose ability to transfer scriptural knowledge, to inspire spiritual commitment and at the same time to shape an unyielding fixation on freedom — if not acquired for themselves, then their posterity — was legendary. Preacher and congregant alike were noted for their fervency in worship style, persistence to gather, and willingness to risk their safety and well-being to meet for worship. Observers of the day commented that it "was nothing strange for them to walk twenty miles on Sunday morning to meeting, and back again at night . . . and that in time of a revival, they were remarkably fond of meeting together, to sing, pray, and exhort, and sometimes preach, and seem to be unwearied in the exercise . . . [placing] more confidence in their own color, than they do in the whites."[19]

---

17. Taylor, *Historical Digest*, ch. 28.

18. Rhys Isaac, *The Transformation of Virginia, 1740-1790* (Chapel Hill, N.C.: University of North Carolina Press, 1982, ch. 13, pp. 300-317

19. L. F. Greene, ed., *Writings of the Late Elder John Leland*, New York: 1845, p. 11.

Belief in a higher power outside of themselves was essential to the survival of African Americans in the era of John Brown's raid on Harpers Ferry. With his military campaign crushed within hours of its launch and Brown's subsequent execution, surely diminished hopes for the freedom they longed for — a major disappointing blow. However, as their repertoire of hymns, spirituals and slave songs continued to reveal throughout the slavery period on plantations near and far, God proved Himself to be their refuge and constant friend while freedom, provision and encouragement — the answers to generations of fervent prayer — materialized as promised.

Verse 2:
Neighbors are kind; I love them everyone.
We get along in sweet accord.
But when my soul needs manna from above
Where could I go but to the Lord?

This photograph is thought to have been taken in 1854 in Shepherdstown, Virginia. The litte girl shown on the left is Mamie, age 6 or 7, a slave in the household of Benjamin Harrison Schley. The Schley home is just across the street from Trinity Episcopal Church whose rector, the Rev. Charles W. Andrews, also presided over the slave congregation of St. Andrew's Episcopal Church. This congregation as freedmen immediately formed an A.M.E. congregation, later becoming the Asbury United Methodist Church of Shepherdstown. (Courtesy of Ben Schley and Dan Riss)

Historic Cowdensville and Winters Lane

COWDENSVILLE, A SMALL, unique community located in southwestern Baltimore County, can trace its origins to a small group of African Americans who were free several decades prior to the Civil War. It has maintained its heritage through eras of slavery, segregation and — most recently — suburban development. And its traditional values — such as family, education, church, work, and community — are still very much alive in Cowdensville today. It is located in Baltimore County, south and west of the general Arbutus area along Sulphur Spring Road at the intersection of Shelbourne Road. The community consists of approximately twenty homes situated on Sulphur Spring Road, Garrett Avenue, Brown's Terrace and Circle Terrace.

Land title searches reveal a Bond of Conveyance issues in September, 1831, from Jacob Counselman a white farmer, to William Barnes of African descent.It transferred to Mr. Barnes ownership of 9½ acres of land known as "Taylor's Forrest," (part of the tract originally a vast estate, consisting of approximately 2000 acres, encompassing much of western Baltimore County.) This document establishes the earliest known transfer of property in this vicinity from white to African ownership, a full thirty years prior to the Civil War.

By 1840, the federal manuscript census records a small group of "free colored persons" between the listings for Edward Levering and Larkin Wade, both white farm owners, in the 1st Collection District of Baltimore County. This small group of African Americans is significant because these families continued to live in Cowdensville for over 150 years: the Garretts, Williams, Scotts, Johnsons, and Matthews.

In 1850 an African American woman named Adeline Hawkins purchased the 9½ acre tract from William Ackwood, his wife Mary, and Martha Barnes. Mary (Barnes) Ackwood and Martha Barnes were sisters who had acquired the property upon the death of their parents, William and Rachel Barnes. The census of 1850 lists the names and ages of family members for the first time, making it possible to link present Cowdensville residents with their ancestors.

In 1851 Adeline Hawkins sold a portion of her property to Hanson Garrett. It encompassed the land east of Sulphur Spring Road and includes the area known today as Garrett Avenue. In 1857 a place of worship was established in a private home on Garrett Avenue. The same home was used

53

The home of Philip Woodland on Winters Lane, shows father Philip with sons Colbert (front) and Charles (on porch). Judging by the 1883 birth date of Charles Woodland, this photo is ca. 1888.

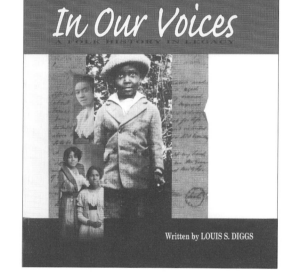

In Our Voices

A FOLK HISTORY IN LEGACY

Written by LOUIS S. DIGGS

The passages on Cowdensville and Winters Lane are taken from *It All Started on Winters Lane* (1995) and *In Our Voices* (1998) by Louis S. Diggs.

as a grammar school for Cowdensville's children.

Authentication of "Cowdensville" as the proper name of the community appears on the cornerstone of the Cowdensville A.M.E. Church, established in 1857. It appears as "Crowdensville" or "Crowdentown" on some maps, such as the *Encyclopædia Britannica* (1911), in which it is placed too far from Arbutus.

The Winters Lane community in Catonsville was started with help from the Freedmen's Bureau in 1867. There was a pioneer family in Catonsville, that of Remus Adams, on Frederick Avenue near Bloomsbury Avenue. He was a blacksmith, first in business with his brother, Samuel Adams, who rented a shop on the property of Richard Bentley, a prominent Quaker in

Montgomery County. Samuel Adams married the sister of James Wesley Hill, known as Canada Jim, who is credited with helping more than 100 slaves escape to freedom in Canada during the late 1850s. Samuel Adams moved to Canada himself in 1859, establishing a blacksmith shop. Certainly the Remus Adams shop was assisting fugitives through Catonsville before the Civil War, even though there is no written documentation. In the 1940s, the son of Samuel Adams, who remained in Canada, spoke of his American uncle as being killed while fighting with the Union Army in the Civil War.

The Adams family, in Canada and in Catonsville, were active members of the African Methodist Episcopal church. The first A.M.E. church in Catonsville is on the corner of Winters Lane and Edmunson Avenue; it was a freedmen's school deeded in perpetuity to the colored people of Catonsville by the Freedman's Bureau, who purchased the corner lot. An A.M.E. congregation formed there, known as St. Johns.

Previously, the closest A.M.E. church was in Oella, a community also known as "Africa," on the inherited farm of the renowned scientist Benjamin Banneker (1731-1806) from his African grandfather, Banneky. The Banneker property is now a Baltimore County park and museum. St. Johns split from the Mt. Gilboa congregation in 1867, because of the large number of freedmen who were settling in Catonsville to work in the lumber industry and other occupations, and could sustain a church closer to their homes. Interestingly, ministers for each congregation were a father and son, the elder Rev. Thomas W. Henry (1794-1877), and younger Rev. John R. Henry (1830–ca.1910, who is listed in "Catonsville P.O" in the census of 1870). A church history lists Rev. John R. Henry as the second minister, from 1870 to 1873, and Rev. John Hubbard as the first settled minister from 1868 to 1870. The building today is a Full Tabernacle Baptist Church. Grace A.M.E., at 67 Winters Lane, is the former St. Johns congregation.

The blacks in Catonsville during the very early years were congenial and very close knit. They became self-sufficient due to segregation and the distance between Catonsville and Baltimore City. They operated their own stores and businesses, and from all accounts, many prospered. Across the street from the freedmen's school and A.M.E. church, there was a building owned by the Catonsville Cooperative Association, a group of black men. Charles Woodland was a member of this Cooperative, and was in the organization of the Prince Hall Masons Landmark Lodge, Temple #40, in 1905, at 48½ Winters Lane.

The Guns of October

Jacob Lawrence, The John Brown series, 1941.
(Courtesy The Detroit Institute of Arts.)

W E WERE FACED with a mystery. Allies for Freedom, a coalition of researchers — named for the late Professor Benjamin Quarles' pioneering book — whose focus is John Brown, became aware of a cache of weapons that had some relationship to Harpers Ferry (Jefferson County, West Virginia). While renovating the family home, Charles Cephas of Catonsville, Maryland, found five antique guns, two of which were stamped with the words "Harper's Ferry." When we contacted Mr. Cephas in July, 1998, he and his mother, Mrs. Lucille Woodland Cephas, agreed to talk with us and allow us to photograph the guns.

During our initial phone conversation, Mr. Cephas said that he found the weapons in the attic of his maternal great-grandfather's home in the historic Winters Lane community. Although two of the long guns had plates indicating that they were made at the arsenal at Harpers Ferry, the family had no ties to the Jefferson County area. Mr. Cephas then shared a very

56

interesting piece of information: his ancestor, Philip Woodland, was among the founders of the Grace African Methodist Episcopal Church of Catonsville, just a few doors away from the family home.

A tie to the Grace A.M.E. Church had enormous significance. When John Brown was arrested, in his captured trunk was his July, 1859, handwritten letter to John Kagi stating "Mr. Thomas Henrie had gone from Hagerstown" and a "trusty man" was needed. Thomas W. Henry was an itinerant minister — twice pastor of the St. James A.M.E. Church in Chambersburg, Pennsylvania, and recent pastor of the antecedent congregation of Grace, the Mt. Gilboa A.M.E. Church, which is located on the historic property of Benjamin Banneker, called "Africa." The Reverend John R. Henry (Thomas Henry's son) served as the first minister of the A.M.E. congregation founded in 1868 in Catonsville, then called St. Johns. Like his father, John R. Henry was suspected of conspiring with John Brown. Although John was not forced to flee Maryland as his father had been, the younger minister was more likely to be connected to the raid. He was stationed at St. James A.M.E. in Havre de Grace at the time of the raid, and was seen in Harrisburg, where Brown's friends were attempting to stage a rescue, in the following weeks.[1]

The house on Winters Lane was built in 1874. It has been continuously in the family's possession since Philip Woodland lived there as early as 1880. What was also interesting was that the house had been the place where traveling ministers stayed when in the area, naturally including the first minister of the congregation, Reverend John R. Henry, who was still an active minister well into the 1900s. Deed records show this house and others nearby changing among family members in cooperative venture.

Another connection between the Woodlands and the Henrys was their tie to St. Mary's County, Maryland. The censuses of 1840 through 1860 reveal Woodland households near that of Thomas Henry's brother, Robert Barnes. Many Woodlands were veterans of U.S.C.T. units that formed in Maryland, as well as members of the A.M.E. Church. We now had a base from which to examine crosscurrents of migration before and after the Civil War.

---

1. Jean Libby, editor, *From Slavery to Salvation: The Autobiography of Rev. Thomas W. Henry of the A.M.E. Church* (1994); "Reverend Thomas W. Henry of Hagerstown" *Negro History Bulletin* 41:4, 1978. WPA records of the churches of Maryland at the State Archives at Annapolis cite Rev. John R. Henry as first settled minister of the St. John's A.M.E. congregation in Catonsville. Union Bethel A.M.E. in nearby Randallstown was mentioned by John Brown as "a good place" to build an army, according to congregation history.

There were other things about the Woodland family and the guns that fit with a pattern of African-American support of the raid. During the interview we also learned that Sarah Woodland started a library for Catonsville blacks in the same schoolhouse and church that was deeded in perpetuity to the community by the Freedmens Bureau, the original St. Johns A.M.E. location at Winters Lane and Edmondson Avenue. Additionally, the Woodland men were Prince Hall Masons.

Our group research signifies that John Brown was building alliances with free blacks who were willing to fight for freedom and were connected with the abolition and emigrationist movements. These free Africans were members of the independent black congregations, were part of the Underground Railroad, and were Prince Hall Masons. They were consistent delegates to Black Conventions which met throughout the free states to petition on behalf of the enslaved, and to declare independence when the Dred Scott decision removed their tenuous citizenship.[2] John Brown knew that this black infrastructure existed because of his own organizational activities for self-defense among fugitives, and recruited support among its most militant members.

We knew there was a relationship between John Brown and Baltimore residents in 1859 — the largest free black community in the country. There were also many people with Baltimore connections who had contact with Brown, including Frederick Douglass, the Reverend William J. Watkins, and his niece, the novelist and poet Frances Watkins. William Watkins and Frances Watkins were heavily implicated with Brown; so much so that William Watkins was suspected of conspiracy and subject to arrest by Virginia immediately after the raid on Harpers Ferry.[3] Frances Watkins wrote to Brown while he was in jail and collected funds from women's groups for the aid of Brown's family, which she personally presented to Mrs. Brown in Philadelphia in November, 1859. Through a Baltimore cousin, Rev. George T. Watkins, the family also directly tied to Rev. Thomas W. Henry.

---

2. The Convention of Colored Men of Ohio, in November , 1858, included William Watkins and Frances Watkins. The delegates approved a resolution which stated "If the Dred Scott dictum be a true exposition of the law of the land, then are the founders of the American Republic convicted by their descendants of base hypocrisy, and colored men are absolved from all allegiance to a government which withdraws all protection."

3. See Benjamin Quarles, *Allies for Freedom; Blacks and John Brown* (1974) for the extent of northern support for Brown's war on slavery. Leroy Graham, *Baltimore: The Nineteenth Century Black Capital* (1988) is most detailed on the Watkins family and on the ties of Masonry and other fraternal organizations with African American leadership.

Could the guns found in the Woodland home in some way be connected to the raid? There are five guns — four long guns and a pistol. Could the rifles have been taken from Harpers Ferry arsenal on October 17, 1859? Could the shotgun and pistol be those which the captured raider John Cook testified had been left in the hands of slaves on the Maryland side of the Potomac River? If any of these possibilities proved true, we would have artifacts which tied the Woodlands directly to the raid and to Harpers Ferry.

The other two long guns were also of interest. One was an antebellum era double-barreled shotgun of foreign make and average quality. The other was quite unusual. It was a fowling piece (bird gun) of pre-war vintage and of foreign make. It was a very expensive, top-of-the-line weapon. On the stock of the gun were the carved initials "G.W." or "J.W.", followed by an "O" which is not an initial. And there was one more interesting marking on the fowling piece. The gun had a small brass or gold plate with an elegantly engraved initial — "W" — indicating the original owner.

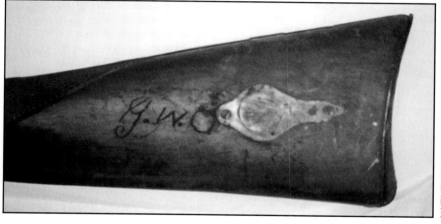

JAMES FISHER

To authenticate the weapons, we went in January 1999 to the National Rifle Association's firearms museum in Fairfax, Virginia. We learned from the curator, Doug Wicklund, that the 1855 model Harpers Ferry rifles were stamped 1860. They were assembled just months too late to be taken from the arsenal at the time of the raid. But each had a rack number in close sequence, indicating they had been stored closely together and therefore were possibly issued to members of the same military unit in the Civil War. The Remington pistol was a 44 caliber, percussion-cap, standard 1863 army issue. Our speculation that this could be the "large army pistol" worn on

John Cook's belt and handed off when he took the Lafayette pistols from the hostage slaveholder Lewis Washington, was wrong.[4]

The curator at the National Firearms Museum, Doug Wicklund, was impressed by the pieces *as a collection*, but did not speculate on that meaning. It was up to Allies for Freedom to develop the paths of the mystery.

Why were there two Harpers Ferry rifles with rack numbers (indicating armory storage) in close sequence. Why was there an expensive fowling piece among the collection of a family of modest means? Who put the brass plate with a "W" on the edge of the stock? What did the presence of the pre Civil War shotgun and a standard-issue 1863 Remington army pistol tell us about Philip Woodland, who was a coachman for wealthy whites in Baltimore and Catonsville? Could we tie these weapons and the Woodland family to Harpers Ferry? Was there a relationship between the Woodland family and known allies of John Brown? We would have to intensify our research.

We began searching the online Soldiers and Sailors database of the National Archives to see if we could locate Woodlands who had connections to the Catonsville house, and who might shed some light on the two Harpers Ferry rifles. We hoped that we had found an explanation for the presence of at least one of the 1860 rifles. There was a Philip Woodland who had served in the 38th United States Colored Troops, who were recruited in St. Mary's County. Could this be our Philip Woodland, settled with his family in Catonsville at the end of the 19th century?

Volunteer research among the military records at the National Archives by Catonsville librarian Julie DeMatteis revealed that the soldier Philip Woodland died in the Civil War. So he could not be the great-grandfather of Charles Cephas, whose grandfather Charles C. Woodland was born in 1883. Closer now, we looked again in the Soldiers and Sailors database and found twenty-three named "Woodland" who served with the Union Army. Six of the Woodlands were in the 19th U.S.C.T., a regiment composed of Africans from Maryland's tidewater and eastern shore regions, and were garrisoned in Harpers Ferry to recruit slaves in the area into army

---

4. There were two Lafayette pistols taken from the Lewis Washington home at the time of the raid. The first Lafayette pistol was captured with John Brown. Cook removed his arms while escaping with four other raiders to seek food at an ironmaking community in Mont Alto, Pennsylvania, where he was captured and brought to Charles Town, tried, and hanged on December 16, 1859. On the first anniversary of John Brown's raid, October 16, 1860, the second Lafayette pistol was returned by mail to Lewis Washington by the head of the National Kansas Committee, Thaddeus Hyatt of N.Y., who had been jailed in Washington, D.C., for refusing to testify before the Senate Committee investigating the Harpers Ferry raid.

service.[5] Among the Woodlands who served in the 19th was William H. Woodland, found to be the brother of Philip Woodland of Catonsville.[6] While the Woodlands who served in the 19th were not all direct line relatives, there is every reason to believe that they knew each other, and were "kin." Three of these Woodlands, including William, transferred to the Navy on the same day, April 17, 1864.

If the Harpers Ferry 1855 rifles belonged to members of the 19th, there are two theories as to how these weapons came into their hands, according to interviews in July, 1999 with Mark Snell, Director of the George Tyler Moore Center for the Study of the Civil War at Shepherd College, and Eric Johnson, an interpretive ranger and weapons expert with the Harpers Ferry National Historical Park. One theory, according to Wicklund and Snell, is that while the 19th was in Harpers Ferry recruiting slaves, they confiscated the weapons from townspeople who had been distributed guns for protection in 1860, after John Brown's raid. Another theory, Johnson's, is that the guns were issued to them while members of the Union Army. Black troops were routinely issued guns thought to be inferior. Model 1855s had "Maynard Tape Systems" as part of their firing device. This system proved to be unreliable and was replaced in subsequent models.

It is possible that the two Harpers Ferry rifles and the Remington pistol belonged to one of the Woodland veterans of the 19th or other Colored units, such as John C. Woodland in the 7th Infantry. We will never know for sure, as the records of the Harpers Ferry armory were burned at the beginning of the Civil War. However, it is most likely that these guns had been in the possession of members of the United States Colored Infantry before being placed in the care of Philip Woodland.

Which leads us to a possible origin of the fowling piece — a possible connection with John Brown's raid. During the raid, on the night of October 17, 1859, Osborne Anderson and Charles Tidd were in the party assigned to capture the slave holder Lewis Washington, the great-grand nephew of George Washington, and take him as a hostage. By the order of John Brown, Anderson (representing the African race) received the sword

5. James H. Rickard [Late Captain 19th U.S. Colored Troops] *Services With Colored Troops in Burnside's Corps* Providence: 1894.

6. The application of the widow of William H. Woodland was attested to by Philip Woodland in 1891, who stated he went to the marriage of his brother William and Mary Edwards on June 5, 1854, "a year after I arrived in Baltimore." The importance of military pension files as family records created by African Americans cannot be overstated.

"The soldiers of the 7th Colored Regiment, who were the first to reach the center of Petersburg on April 2 [1865], and those of the 9th and 19th Regiments who were in the forefront of Union troops to enter the burning city of Richmond a few days later, had every reason to feel proud of their achievement." James H. Whyte, historian of Maryland. (Photo courtesy National Technical Information Service, Springfield, Virginia.)

that had been presented to George Washington by Frederick the Great of Prussia.

The group also confiscated a pair of pistols presented to George Washington by Lafayette, a wagon, a carriage (whose enslaved coachman Jim would die in the Shenandoah River), and two guns — a double-barreled shotgun and a foreign-made fowling piece. Could the fowling gun found in Catonsville be that belonging to Lewis Washington? The double-barreled shotgun from the Washington plantation had been buried by a slave and then recovered, Lewis Washington told a Senate investigating committee six months after the raid. Osborne Anderson and Charles Tidd escaped, separately, meeting with great surprise in Cleveland in November. Might one of them still be holding the Washington gun? It was Charles Tidd who armed the enslaved and free Africans in Maryland. He had discarded two Sharps' rifles and a drill manual for a guerilla army given him by John Brown outside Chambersburg while escaping, probably to avoid discovery after Cook was captured at Mont Alto.[7]

---

7. [Chambersburg] *Valley Spirit*, November 2, 1859.

"Washington as Colonel of the Virginia Regiment 1772" by Charles Willson Peale. Peale was known for his attention to detail. It is interesting to note that Washington is in military dress, yet wished to be commemorated with his fowling piece, instead of with a military weapon.

The fowling piece was never found. The wagon which was taken from the Washington plantation to Maryland was pointed out by returning slaves who made the choice to remain in Virginia rather than chance being hunted with the fleeing survivors.

Could this be the missing fowling piece, last seen "in the hands of a Negro" on the Maryland side of the river? What we do know is that the fowling piece is similar to the description of the missing Washington gun, that a "W" on a brass plate to indicate ownership is consistent with the practice of some of the Washingtons in Jefferson County. It is highly unlikely that the Woodlands would have spent such a sum on a personal weapon, although it could have been a gift from a wealthy German merchant in Maryland, Gustav Lurman, Sr., for whom Philip Woodland worked as a coachman. So what of the last gun — the double-barreled shotgun? The Woodland family has a history of civic activism.[8] Just after the Civil War, the Woodland home in Baltimore was located at 38 Orchard

---

8. John C. Woodland, likely cousin of Philip Woodland and a leader of a Baltimore veteran's group of the GAR (Grand Army of the Republic), was also associated with an entrepreneurial Christian (mainly Baptist) lodge-based organization, the United Galilean League of Fishermen. The African American Community Association of Jefferson County, West Virginia, is restoring a building in Charles Town that dates from 1890 ownership by the United Galilean League of Fishermen. Completion is anticipated early in the 21st century.

Street — near the "Black Fifth Avenue!"[9] In the 1890s, Mrs. Sarah Lee Woodland founded one of the first libraries open to blacks in Baltimore in the schoolhouse and church on Winters Lane, where their daughter, Mary, was now a teacher. Two other Woodland children, Colbert and Charles, also became school teachers. Catonsville Woodlands were among the early members of the rapidly-growing NAACP, with its strong community base.

Leroy Graham, author of *Baltimore: The Nineteenth Century Black Capital*, believes that armed self-defense organizations were returning at the turn of the century because of the rise of lynchings and state sanctioned segregation. Charles Cephas, Jr. remembers his grandfather, Charles Woodland having the Remington pistol in his desk. It is not a stretch of imagination to believe the patriarch of this family would gather such a collection for the purpose of protecting his family and community, as well as preserving history. Philip may have owned the shotgun even before the Civil War, when it was illegal for him to do so, for such protection.

Allies for Freedom believes that the weapons, taken collectively and placed in the context of 19th century Baltimore, can be assessed. The guns were left for another generation to find and to tell a story of those brave Africans who were willing to fight for freedom. They were left in honor of John Brown, as a reminder of his sacrifice. The collection in its setting reveals that here was a family who were actively engaged in the Civil Rights movement of the 19th and early 20th centuries.

There is one more intriguing piece of information which bolsters our conclusions. Lucille Woodland Cephas was apologetic that she could not remember more. The old folks did not talk too much about the old days and she was a younger child. She wished that her older brother were still alive because he knew more. But she did remember some of the stories that had been handed down in this proud family. And she remembered something else. Even though travel was expensive and very difficult for African Americans when she was a child, there was one place that her parents nevertheless felt was important for the family to visit: Harpers Ferry.

---

9. When the Fifteenth Amendment to the United States Constitution, which guaranteed universal manhood suffrage, was ratified in 1870, the largest celebration in the nation took place in Baltimore, with over 20,000 people participating. As part of the celebration a grand parade marched through the city. The parade route included Orchard Street. See "The Story of the 15th Amendment in Maryland" by David Troy on the web site of the Maryland State Archives.

The Woodlands of Maryland

The issues surrounding African American support for John Brown in 1859 brought a single family into focus because it was in their family home where potential artifacts of the John Brown raid were discovered. The Harpers Ferry rifles relate to family members in the Civil War, and were probably retained because of John Brown's association with the town. The older civilian weapons are still under study.

Examining the puzzles of genealogical relationship are larger than a single family because of the nature of slavery in Maryland, bounty payments to slaveholders and slaves during the Civil War (but not for free enlistees and draftees), and the emancipation of all those legally enslaved in the state on November 1, 1864.

The Woodland family in America were centered in St. Mary's County, Maryland, but were also found in Charles, Prince George's and Calvert counties. Our research focuses on the generation which was born in the 1830s to 1840s, and moved to Baltimore during the 1850s and 1860s. Their marriages in the next generation mingled other notable free African Maryland families, specifically the Butlers, a black family that extended into many Maryland counties in considerable numbers on the censuses. The name Woodland as a surname appears in slave records, an event that signifies that there were often manumission conditions, in previous agreement with the slaveholders, which was common in Maryland. The Woodlands of Maryland were bound to a closely related group of St. Mary's County and Charles County farmers and physicians. Those family names were Barber, Yates, Harris, Reeder, and Gardiner. As there was only one instance of a white Woodland who married into their group, it does not seem likely that the name generated from a white plantation unless it was during the Colonial period. It is more likely that the name "Woodland" was chosen by the family to recognize each other, and that it refers to a location, an actual woodland, in their occupations of the early 1800s. The occupation of two generations of the specific Woodlands of our study in Baltimore soon after the Civil War was as wood sawyers. This type of clan identification, based also upon occupation, is culturally West African.

As persons with the name Woodland gradually became free, the family identity grew. It may be seen by the following fugitive advertisement for Lewis Woodland of Charles County on December 2, 1859, that such family identification was a survival technique. The group of slaveholding families were trading the Woodlands among each other without regard to families remaining together. Records of Lewis Woodland's parentage were kept so that he could be quickly searched for:

$150 REWARD. Ran away from the subscriber, living in Piccawaxen, Charles County, Md., on the night of the 1st instant, a NEGRO MAN, who calls himself Lewis Woodland. He is the property of V. Barber, under 22 years of age, of medium height say about 5 ft. 8 to 9 inches, and of a light black or chestnut color. He has relations in St. Mary's County, a father at Colonel Forbes, in Prince George's, a mother at Mr. Jonathan Y. Barber's in Calvert, and he may endeavor to pass in either direction.

I will give fifty dollars for his apprehension in either Charles or St. Mary's county, one hundred dollars if taken in Prince George's or Calvert county, or one hundred fifty dollars if taken elsewhere. In either case to be secured so that I can get him again.

H. R. Harris, Allens Fresh Post Office, December 2, 1859.

The related male Woodlands of our study were among the "relations in St. Mary's County" that Lewis was expected to seek. One, John C. Woodland, was enslaved to "V. Barber", Violetta Harris Barber, the widow of Dr. Luke Philip Barber. According to his pension file statement, made in 1899, he was

"born in Charles County, near Allens Fresh P.O. on Jany 8, 1839, and was a slave under Dr. Philip Barber. At the age of 13 years I was taken to St. Mary's Co Md., and lived near Oakville P.O. as a slave under Elizabeth Reader (daughter of Dr. Philip Barber). I enlisted in the army in Sept. 1863 When I returned from the army in Nov 1866, I went to St. Mary's Co Md and located near Chaptico P.O. remained there about three years & came to Balto Md in 1869."

The census of 1870 in Baltimore shows Philip Woodland, age 30, his wife Sarah, 25 (who was the daughter of Charles C. Lee of St. Mary's County), their three children ages 7, 4, and 2. Three adult males named Woodland were in the household: Cornelius, 65 (the father of Philip), Washington, laborer, 41,

National Archives Pension Record

and John, a hod carrier, 25. Philip was a coachman (his lifelong occupation), and Cornelius a sawyer.[11] John Woodland in the census was six years younger than the date which John C. Woodland named as his birth, but there is a connection of occupation: a young man named Cooper Hawkins lived in the house, and his business was driving a cart, which is the occupation that John C. Woodland and others cite in his pension file, operating a delivery business and laying carpets. John C. Woodland was the head of a veterans group, and active in the United Galilean League of Fisherman, who assisted his widow, Susan Hawkins Woodland, when he died at Riggs Avenue in Baltimore (a Catonsville Woodland family property) in 1917.

In 1880, Cornelius Woodland was living at 35 Greenwillow Street, with another son, William H. Woodland, his wife Mary E., and six children. Both were woodsawyers. In the most remarkable document of our research, Philip Woodland testified to the Pensions Board in 1891 that "William H. Woodland who was my brother, and this claimant Mary Edwards _____ were married by Rev. Mr. Wylie In St. Mary's Co Md in 1854. I remember the exact date as it just one year after I came to Balto and that was in 1853." William H. Woodland was a veteran of the 19th Infantry, U.S. Colored Troops, organized at Camp Stanton in Benedict, Maryland. According to his military records, he was thirty-three when he enlisted, a free man and a farmer. Five other men named Woodland were in the 19th Infantry, which recruited for slaves in Charles Town, and Harpers Ferry, West Virginia, in late March, 1864.

It is evident from this document that his move to Baltimore in 1853, when he was thirteen years old, was a key event in Philip Woodland's life. Philip was not in the military in the Civil War; his marriage to Sarah Lee took place about 1863. Who his employer was as a coachman in Baltimore until after 1870 is not yet known, but in the 1870s he moved to Catonsville and was listed in the census of 1880 at the estate of the widow of Gustav Lurman, Sr., a wealthy antislavery German immigrant merchant who had a business on Franklin Street in Baltimore with Henry Oelrichs in 1860.

---

11. The census data are combined with military records, wills, death certificates, and other sources researched by Julie DeMatteis of the Baltimore County Public Library in Catonsville. Interpretation of these data with the interview of Charles Cephas and Lucille Woodland Cephas as consistent with manumission for brothers William and Philip Woodland before general emancipation in Maryland in November, 1964, is by the editor, Jean Libby, the author, Hannah N. Geffert, and researcher, Julie DeMatteis. John C. Woodland was manumitted by presidential order upon enlistment in the 7th Colored Infantry in an area where great physical resistance was made by the slaveholders, including the murder of a white recruiting officer.

Philip Woodland was also enumerated on the 1880 census in Catonsville as head of his own household (he is listed twice). They were living in the house on Winters Lane where the artifacts were found.

The slaveholder Dr. Thomas Barber, in St. Mary's County, listed William, Philip, and Washington on the Maryland Slave Statistics prepared in 1867. Barber received a $100 "compensation" for the loss of William, although none for Philip (who "left" on the same day William enlisted in the 19th Infantry, January 5, 1864), or Washington, who "left" in May.

There is no evidence that William H. Woodland requested, or received, such a bounty for military service as a slave.[12] According to his widow's pension application, the soldier lived near Charlotte Hall Post Office when he enlisted in January, 1864. After his service at Harpers Ferry and the Shenandoah Valley, William H. Woodland served on four ships of the United States Navy., which did not have segregated units.

---

12. The bounty to slave recruits, and compensation for slaveholders in Maryland for their manumission is described in John C. Blassingame, "The Recruitment of Negro Troops in Maryland" (*Maryland Historical Magazine*, v. 58, no. 1, March, 1963). Free persons who enlisted or were drafted were not given this bounty.

Charlotte Hall, Allens Fresh, and Chaptico are located in Charles and St. Mary's counties. The 1st, 7th and 19th Colored Infantries formed in Benedict (Camp Stanton). (*Johnson's New Illustrated Family Atlas of the World*, 1865.)

70

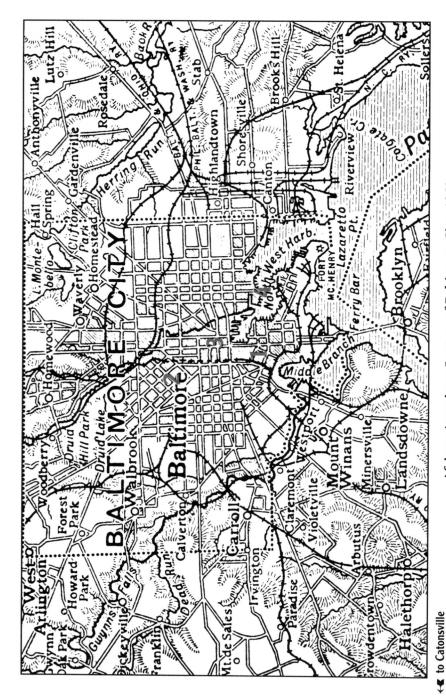

African American Centers of Baltimore City, 1859

to Catonsville

This map gathers the congregations and communities of African Americans in Baltimore City into sections which demonstrate the proximity of activist institutions and people. The base map (*Encyclopædia Britannica*, 1911) does not depict every street for the time period of 1859/1860, nor are all black neighborhoods portrayed. All churches named were predominantly African.

1. **SOUTHSIDE: Vibrant enclave of black community leaders, Quakers, and other anti- slavery activists.** This is the Sharp Street-Leadenhall area, whose flagship is the Sharp Street Methodist Episcopal church and school. It includes Peach Alley, the Tabernacle of the Grand Order of the United Galilean League of Fishermen, founded by Hemsley Nichols in 1856.

2. **ORCHARD STREET: Denominational crossroads of urban activism and style.** Historic Orchard Street Church (both M.E. and A.M.E) restored, is now the Baltimore headquarters of the National Urban League. Madison Avenue Presbyterian Church, Rev. Hiram Revels, and his residence at 41 Tyson Street. Woodland family residence at 38 Orchard in 1868-70; Oblate Sisters of Providence maintained a school at Richmond, near Park. St. John A.M.E. Mission began here in 1855, Rev. Henry McNeal Turner the traveling minister by 1860. The school of Rev. George T. Watkins was at Orchard and Tessier Streets.

3. **DOWNTOWN: Center of independent Methodists, Baptists and Roman Catholics.** This is the dynamic core of enterprise, the Underground Railroad, tradespeople, and entrepreneurs; Bethel A.M.E. (on Saratoga, near Gay), Roman Catholic congregation (St. Mary's County origin) St. Francis Xavier at Calvert and Pleasant; St. James Protestant Episcopal Church, North and Saratoga. Little Monument Street (where Rev. Thomas W. Henry received aid in escaping Baltimore in 1859); market area is now Lexington Market; First Colored Baptist on Thompson near Forrest; Asbury Methodist Episcopal at East and Douglass Streets (street name present here before used as a possible UGRR signal by Frederick Bailey).

4. **EASTSIDE: Baltimore Center of the enslaved Frederick Bailey (later Douglass).** The Dallas Street Methodist Episcopal Church (later called Centennial), on Strawberry Alley in 1859 (Rev. William Watkins was circuit minister there for a time), about five blocks from the President Street Railway Station, from which Frederick Bailey (later Douglass) made his escape from bondage in 1838. Frederick Bailey went to school here, after also attending Bethel A.M.E.'s school. He purchased property in the vicinity in later years, renting the houses. It is in the City Docks area, where he was a ship caulker. In 1870, African American workers on the docks petitioned Congress to relieve racial discrimination. They were aided by Senator Hiram Revels of Mississippi, a minister in Baltimore in 1859.

Hiram and Willis Revels, Lewis Leary, and John Copeland

WHEREVER ALLIES FOR FREEDOM have searched for connections among African friends of John Brown, the clues often lead to relatives. Among the whites, it is well known that three of Brown's sons were in the Harpers Ferry raid (two were killed, one escaped), the Coppoc brothers, Quakers from Iowa, and the Thompson brothers, New York mountain neighbors whose children intermarried with those of John Brown.

Among blacks, the uncle and nephew relationship of Lewis Leary and John Copeland, from triracial families in North Carolina who had migrated to Ohio, is also well known. They and other relatives became active in rescues of fugitives and in the growing Convention Movement seeking self-determination.

It is a discovery of our research that Hiram Revels, who would become the first elected United States senator of African descent, was the first cousin of Lewis Leary, who died in the battle of Harpers Ferry. The Reverend Hiram Revels was a minister living on Tyson Street in Baltimore in 1859, pastor of the Madison Avenue Presbyterian congregation. It was founded by white Presbyterians for the enslaved of their households in 1847, and

Lewis Leary   Hiram Revels   John Copeland

The portraits of Lewis Leary and John Copeland, who died fighting with John Brown, are from Richard Hinton, *John Brown and His Men* (1894); Hiram Revels is from Carter G. Woodson, *The Negro in Our History* (1922).

attracted many African Baltimoreans among the growing free population because of his intellectual manner.

The North Carolina origins of these relatives is relevant to the way in which they became leaders in the civil rights movement of the 1850s which was centered in the midwest, and to whom John Brown came looking for support for his war on slavery. They were triracial Americans, with an African/Indian/European identity. Information on the family relationship comes from a descendant, Matthew Leary Perry, published in 1950, researched by Rhonda Williams of the Cumberland County Information Center. The first clues we followed appeared as a note in Benjamin Quarles, *Allies for Freedom*.

While the evidence of cousin relationship would indicate that the future senator Rev. Hiram Revels knew of John Brown's raid in advance, the evidence that we prefer to look at is his record of social activism before and during the Civil War. From his pulpit in Baltimore, Hiram Revels recruited two regiments of African soldiers into the Union forces in 1863 (following the Emancipation Proclamation) — the 4th and 39th United States Colored Troops.

At the same time, Revels interacted with new A.M.E. minister Henry McNeal Turner, who was pastor of the St. John Mission in the city as the refugee population increased.[1] In 1864, the Rev. Hiram Revels replaced Turner at Bethel A.M.E. in Leavenworth, Kansas. Rev. Turner returned to Washington and recruited the 1st USCT Infantry in Maryland, becoming its chaplain.

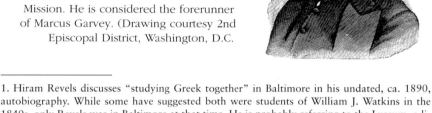

Henry McNeal Turner was a South Carolinian who became Bishop of the A.M.E. Church after serving in the Georgia legislature during Reconstruction. He became a strong African emigrationist because of mistrust of America, and founded the A.M.E. South African Mission. He is considered the forerunner of Marcus Garvey. (Drawing courtesy 2nd Episcopal District, Washington, D.C.

---

1. Hiram Revels discusses "studying Greek together" in Baltimore in his undated, ca. 1890, autobiography. While some have suggested both were students of William J. Watkins in the 1840s, only Revels was in Baltimore at that time. He is probably referring to the Lyceum, a library and lecture series organization in which he was active. Revels and Turner were in Baltimore and Washington D.C. together from 1860 to 1862.

Dr. Willis Revels medically examined the Indiana recruits of the 28th USCT, sent to Ellicott City and Baltimore for hundreds of additions to the Union Army. The doctor-minister became pastor of Bethel A.M.E. Church in Baltimore in 1870. His brother Hiram Revels went to Mississippi following the Civil War, changing to the Methodist Episcopal denomination because that was the mission group among the freedmen. Assisting Africans from slavery was clearly their priority. Following the Civil War, Hiram Revels became active in restructuring the Constitution of the state of Mississippi to include the proportionally largest African population of the country. In 1870, the Rev. Hiram R. Revels was elected by the legislature to serve the unexpired term of Jefferson Davis in the United States Senate, created when he resigned to become the president of the Confederacy.

Cleveland was the meeting place for John Brown with the militant slave-rescuers, John Copeland and Lewis Leary. He recruited them for Harpers Ferry at a lecture they attended. He was already in touch with emigrationist and abolitionist leaders there: James M. Langston and Charles H. Langston, and another North Carolinian, James Henry Harris. It is Harris who attended the Chatham Convention in 1858, promised aid, and assisted the escaping Harpers Ferry raider Osborne Anderson. During the Civil War, Harris helped recruit the 28th Infantry USCT in Indiana, along with Dr. Willis Revels, the examining physician. He was probably present when half the regiment was raised in Ellicott City and Baltimore in 1864.

After the war, James Henry Harris returned to his native North Carolina, and became active in politics, along with John Leary, the younger brother of the martyred Lewis. His career included appointment as a commissioner of Raleigh, and establishment of an institution for the deaf and blind. James Henry Harris, like so many of the African activists of the time, was also a builder. He established the Land and Development Company, founded a community named Oberlin (for the abolitionist Ohio college), and loaned money for mortgages for the purchase of homes in new communities after the Civil War. The North Carolina-to-Ohio pathway of free African emigrants brought them into contact with John Brown and the Underground Railroad organizations, both black and white.

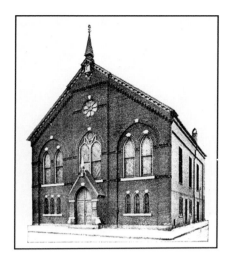

The Madison Street Presbyterian Church was organized in a Mission School in 1842, obtaining this building from white Baptists in 1848. Hiram Revels was the first African pastor, serving from 1858 through 1864. Significantly, the previous pastor, was a white abolitionist missionary. Revels, who assisted and then replaced him in Baltimore, attended the Presbyterian Seminary in Galesburg, Illinois and Lane Seminary in Ohio. The congregation moved to Madison Avenue, in 1927. They continue to be a socially active ministry, addressing African concerns in the city. (Photo courtesy the African American Collection, Enoch Pratt Library.)

St. John A.M.E. Church, organized 1855 in a blacksmith shop on Tessier Street. Ministers in the 1860s included the Rev. Henry M. Turner, a strong African emigrationist and a chaplain during the Civil War. The Rev. George T. Watkins created a school for young free Africans here before the Civil War. The Mission may have been the "St. John" recruiting station for USCT regiments. This church was constructed in 1869; congregation is now located on Carrollton Avenue in Baltimore. (Photo courtesy 2nd Episcopal District, Washington, D.C.

The Oblate Sisters of Providence in Baltimore are the first group of African American women religious, refugees from San Domingo (Haiti) during the Revolution of the 1790s. They built an academy and seminary on Richmond Street in 1836, at times the only place of worship for Baltimore's numerous black Catholics. In 1857, the Jesuits established a chapel in the basement of St. Ignatious Church on Calvert Street; by 1863 the independent St. Frances Xavier Church was built. (Photo courtesy Josephite Father Peter E. Hogan.)

The Nationalist and the Revolutionary:
Martin R. Delany and John Brown

HONORABLE MAYOR, WHATEVER ideas of liberty I may have, have been received from reading the lives of your revolutionary fathers. I have therein learned that a man has a right to defend his castle with his life, even unto the taking of life. Sir, my house is my castle; in that castle are none but my wife and my children, as free as the angels of heaven, and whose liberty is as sacred as the pillars of God. If any man approaches that house in search of a slave — I care not who he may be, whether constable or sheriff, magistrate or even judge of the Supreme Court — nay, let it be he who sanctioned this act to become law (President Millard Fillmore) surrounded by his cabinet as his bodyguard, with the Declaration of Independence waving above his head as his banner, and the Constitution of his country upon his breast as his shield, — if he crosses the threshold of my door, and I do not lay him a lifeless corpse at my feet, I hope the grave may refuse my body a resting place, and righteous heaven my spirit a home. Oh, No! He cannot enter that house and we both live.

Martin R. Delany
Reponse to the Fugitive Slave Act
Allegheny Pennsylvania, September 30, 1850

Chatham, Canada West,
Capitol of the African Emigrationist Community

It is the winter of 1855-56, and winters in Canada are always cold — there is no reason to imagine this season was any different. But cold or not, in February 1856, Martin Delany, wife Catherine (now pregnant) and their three children, Toussant, Charles, and Alexandre, will leave their Pittsburgh, Pennsylvania community called "Hayti," where he has worked for the last 25 years, and settle in Chatham. There are approximately 2,400 Africans living within the city limits of Chatham, and hundreds more on farms in surrounding Kent County. Most were fugitives from enslavement in America. Not only were they free, but this was virgin country with thousands of acres of timbered and watered land selling for $2.50 per acre.

We are pleased to state to our readers, the arrival of our esteemed and talented friend, Dr. M.R. Delany of Pittsburgh, Pa. in this town, yesterday morning, who intends making this his home. It would be useless to attempt to acquaint many of our readers of the character of the Doctor, as a physician, having been long in practice and thoroughly known by all the professional men of the states and the inhabitants, generally; and as a writer, and orator is distinguished among the number that now occupy the field, in the distribution of knowledge for the elevation and improvement of mankind, which is certainly commendatory to all friends of progress here and elsewhere. The Doctor proposes to resume the practice of medicine immediately, when he will doubtless be at his office on William Street, east of King.

Provincial Freeman

During his first year in Chatham, Delany lived and worked from the Villia Mansion on William Street, an early hotel patronized by the African community. His medical practice was much welcomed and much needed so that by February of the new year he was able to pay $1,800 outright for a house on Murray Street on one acre of land on the north bank of the Thames River.

But it's more than the practice of medicine that brought Delany to Canada in the winter. Delany has given up the fight for faith in America in particular, and faith in whites, in general. Victor Ullman says: "Delany began to lose his illusions concerning freedom in America by 1838, the year that Frederick Douglass escaped slavery."

The 1850 Fugitive Slave Act left little doubt in Delany's mind that "We must have position, independent of anything pertaining to white men and nations." By 1854 he had set out to establish that position with the call for an Emigration Convention for nation-forming in Cleveland, Ohio.

The 1850 Fugitive Slave Act had shaken faith in white Americans from the hearts of the free African community, and Delany would provide the ideological glue that gave meaning to the call for a nationalist/activist gathering, instead of just another "wishful debate."

The glue was found on the pages of his hastily-penned 1852 book, *The Condition, Elevation, Emigration and Destiny of the Colored People of the United States, Practically Considered*. Ullman notes: "Very soon in Pittsburgh, Delany found that he was far from alone. His book had been a bugle call among his people — heard among the unheard and unknown — and there emerged during 1853 and 1854 new names, new voices, new attitudes, and new leaders among the free Negroes."

This was the second nationalist convention among Africans in North America. The first met in Toronto in 1851, called by Henry Bibb and addressed by Delany. Between these two nationalist conventions, Frederick Douglass called the National Colored Convention in Rochester in July

1853, which resulted in asking — as had all conventions before — the American government for rights, for suffrage, for citizenship . . . *How many times do you ask the same people (your oppressors, enslavers) for the same thing, before you are considered a beggar?* Delany's position was: "I am weary of our miserable condition, and am heartily sick of whining and sniveling at the feet of white men, *begging* for their refuse, and often existing by mere sufferance."

We need to note that Douglass — the father of the integrationist ideology, as Delany is called the father of nationalist ideology — was unable to draw a quorum for the January 1854 follow-up meeting, and by 1855 the National Convention of Colored Men was stamped a lost cause, not to meet again until after the Civil War. The growing differences between the two men were evident — in 1847 they edited *The North Star* together; in 1848 they chaired the Colored National Convention, with Douglass elected president.

Delany did not attend Douglass's Rochester Convention in 1853, and Douglass did not attend the Cleveland Emigration Convention, and verbally condemned the gathering. The African abolitionist movement had come apart at the seams, and the fault was laid at Delany's door.

Delany's Nationalist Convention made it — in a favorite phrase of the late Kwame Ture — "crystal clear" that this was an emigrationist convention, and all of the opposite mindset need not apply. The Convention's opening act was the selection of a Credentials Committee composed of: Rev. William Webb, Pittsburgh; James T. Holly, New York; Rev. Augustus Green, Cincinnati; H. Ford Douglas, Louisiana; and William Lambert, Michigan. Each aspiring delegate was asked two questions:

1) Are you in favor of emigration?
2) Do you subscribe to the objects and sentiments contained in the call for a National Emigration Convention, and will you do all in your power to carry out the same?

The Convention seated 106 delegates from ten of the United States and Canada — delegates with one agenda, emigration. The vital questions before the body were to build the organization, raise the funds, and establish the homeland.

Delany, whose book brought many of the delegates together, had some answers for these questions. Building on Delany's ideas the 1854 Convention formed a National Board of Commissioners as a governing body, and established a quarterly periodical the *African American Repository* as a literary and scientific journal to document African genius and intellect. Committees for Domestic Relations, Financial Relations, and Foreign Relations were formed, and a special Office of Foreign Secretary was established. Three exploration committees to look into emigration sites were organized: Africa, Martin Delany; Haiti, Theodore Holly; Central America, James Whitfield. The Convention had, in essence, established the rudiments of a government. In fact, H. Ford Douglas would later remark of the proceedings as "the making of a colored nationality."

One of the most significant aspects of the 1854 Emigration Convention was the role women played. Women voted, argued fine points of resolutions, served on committees, and were elected to office. Mary E. Bibb, whose husband, Henry, called the 1851 Convention, was elected second vice-president. Four other women were elected to the permanent Finance Committee. Ullman notes:

> Within one month all of the departments were in operation. Within five years the emigrationists (nationalists) had a black-financed organization sponsoring its periodical and three distinct parties of exploration. In April, 1861, when Fort Sumter was fired upon, Martin Delany was awaiting a trained nucleus of the first colony to be created in Abeokuta, on the West coast of Africa (current-day Nigeria).

At this point Delany had called and carried through the only successful convention ever held, state or national, by the African community. A group of African institutions, African manned and African financed made Delany, at this juncture, the international leader of the African community in Canada and America. Is it any wonder that John Brown was directed to Martin Delany as the one man who had the power?

ALLIES FOR FREEDOM

William Lambert from *The Black West,*
William Loren Katz

William Lambert (1820-1892) of Detroit, organizer of the African Mysteries, Men of Oppression, a militant fraternal organization that operated the Underground Railroad in the area. Lambert, an active participant in John Brown's May 1858 convention in Chatham, was associated with George de Baptiste, another major Underground Railroad leader.

Henry Bibb (1813-1854), fugitive from Kentucky, began the first periodical among the Canadian emigres, *The Voice of the Fugitive*, which was the periodical of emigrationists. His own memoir of escape, considered one of the best, was published in 1849 with the assistance of his wife, Mary Miles of Boston, another emigrationist leader, who carried on his work at the Convention of 1855 after Bibb's untimely death at the age of forty-one.

Henry Bibb, *Narrative of the Life and Adventures of Henry Bibb*

By Any Means Necessary

IT IS APRIL of 1858, and we would imagine a brisk spring day, typical of Chatham, Canada West. Martin Delany, the doctor, is in the country, checking patients, visiting friends and carrying on his "country doctor duties." But his concentration is really on his African tour, and his responsibilities as leader of the Niger Valley Exploring Party. Where will he get the money? Who will be in the Party? When will they leave?

As he rides and thinks, enjoying the fresh brisk air on his face, back in Chatham, Catherine Delany is receiving an unexpected visitor.[1]

"Yes, Sir, what is it you want?"

"Good morning, Madam, I wish to speak with Dr. Martin Delany."

When told the doctor is not at home — may she take a message? — the gentleman hesitates for a moment, unconsciously stroking his long white beard, and replies, "No, no, but do tell him that I will return in two weeks' time."

Catherine is not able to obtain any information about the stranger, and Delany has other things on his mind: his African tour. The visit is passed off as just another person with a passing pain looking for the doctor.

But, such was not the case, for on time, in two weeks, the visitor called again. And again, the doctor was away. "Tell Dr. Delany I will call him again in four days and that it is most urgent that I speak with him."

The tone of the man's voice, the determination in his face, left no doubt in Catherine's mind of the seriousness of the stranger's visit. When Delany returned she took the time to explain the visit, describing in detail the stranger's appearance: He was an older white man, with a long beard and grey hair. There was a kind of sad, placid countenance about him and he spoke with a solemn, serious tone.

"He said he would return in fours days and that he must see you!"

This time the stranger is not passed off, but is awaited. As the four days pass they find Delany moving hurriedly along Murray Street to keep his appointment. Two other men are also moving along the street. Based on Catherine's description he recognizes one as the mysterious visitor. As he

---

1. Conversations are verbatim from Frank (Frances) A. Rollin, *Life and Public Services of Martin R. Delany*, (Boston: Lee & Shepherd, 1883).

stops the man and inquires if he is the visitor, the other steps forward saying,

"This is Captain John Brown."

"Not Captain John Brown of Osawatomie?"

"I am, Sir." "And you . . . ?"

"Dr. Delany, Dr. Martin R. Delany, Sir," pushing his hand forward, surprised and delighted to meet John Brown on the streets of Chatham. And looking for him, no less!

"Sir, I have come to Chatham expressly to see you, this being my third visit on the errand. I must see you at once, Sir," and he leaned forward with quiet emphasis, "And that, too, in private, as I have much to do and but little time before me. If I am to do nothing here I want to know it at once."

Delany noted: "We went directly to the private parlor of a nearby hotel." Here Brown spoke of "his great scheme of Kansas emigration," (no mention of Harpers Ferry) which, to be successful, "must be aided and countenanced by the influence of a general [African] convention or council." This he was unable to effect in the United States, but had been advised by distinguished mutual friends that if he could contact Delany "his object would be obtained."

But Delany is still confused. Africans have been holding conventions for the past twenty years, why come all this way to Canada just for a convention? "Because," replied Brown, "the people of the northern states are cowards; slavery has made cowards of them all. The whites are afraid of each other and the blacks are afraid of the whites. You can effect nothing among such people," Brown added, Delany notes, "with decided emphasis!"

And the "distinguished friends who sent Brown to see Delany, who might they be? Delany does not say, and other writers only mention briefly the Brown-Delany meeting of April, 1858.

It's probable they were leaders in the African Abolitionist Movement and the Underground Railroad. Topping the list would be Frederick Douglass, followed by Bishop J.W. Loguen of Syracuse; Lewis Hayden of Boston; Dr. James McCune Smith and William Still of Philadelphia; and the Reverend Henry Highland Garnet of New York.[2]

If these were "the distinguished friends," then who were the cowards Brown spoke of? A clue appears in Brown's reply to Delany on the need for a council outside the United States:

---

2. All these men are documented with associations to John Brown, see Benjamin Quarles, *Allies for Freedom; Blacks and John Brown* (1974).

"It is men that I want, not money; money I can get plentiful enough, but no men. Money can come without being seen, but men are afraid of identification with me, though they favor my methods."

We must remember that, at this time, John Brown had a price on his head, and that the abolitionist movement had undergone, at a minimum, a three-way split. The white element is factionalized, Delany has siphoned the emigrationist/nationalist Africans, and Douglass remains in a disintegrating persuasionist movement, the National Negro Convention, in which his own leadership is in question.

That persuasionist element is in denial of the Fugitive Slave Laws of 1793 and 1850 as well as the Dred Scott decision of 1857. They still believe they are citizens and America has a conscience, and they cannot jeopardize that "believed citizenship" by casting their lot with a "wanted killer" against slavery like Brown.

Listen closely, hear the Malcolm-Martin arguments of the 1960s. Martin says, "We must struggle in such a fashion so that after we win they will still accept us." Malcolm says, "An eye for an eye, a tooth for a tooth, a head for a head, and we carry this off by any means necessary, that is the only thing America understands."

Listening to Brown's plans for expanding the Underground Railroad operation to a more militant level, backing that up with armed and trained African revolutionaries, Delany could not help but see parallels between Brown's scheme and the organization of William Lambert and George DeBaptiste, the African Mysteries. Brown's closest African companion, Richard Richardson, who recently joined his white jayhawker band, became (or perhaps was already) a part of the African Mysteries.[3]

On May 8th, the day before John Brown's 58th birthday, Alfred Whipper unlocked the door to the schoolhouse on Princess Street. Slowly, casually men strolled, chatted, and greeted each other until within the hour that twelve white men and sixty or seventy Africans filled the classroom. To offset suspicions of the curious, Delany had let it be known that a biracial Masonic meeting was in order.

When Frederick Douglass had failed to attract a follow-up for the 1853 Convention and thereby lost his attempt to build an organization (the National Council), he also lost a level of leadership of the "Free African Community." In 1858, Delany is, without a doubt, "the man to see."

3. A letter from Richard Realf to John Brown, May 31, 1858. The Kansas State Historical Society has the original letter to "Dear Uncle" in the John Brown Collection.

However, we must wonder if Brown really understood this Delany-Douglass, Martin-Malcolm, integrationist-nationalist schism that has plagued African people since our unwitting arrival on these shores.

The Convention was called to order by Mr. John Jackson, on whose motion Reverend William Munro was elected president. John Kagi (of Brown's guerilla army) was elected secretary on Brown's motion. On a motion from Delany, Brown was introduced to the Convention. All had heard and read of Brown the revolutionary, and here, in the flesh, was Brown the man. The whispering ceased, the cross conversations stopped, the room fell silent as Delany gave praise to Captain John Brown, his exploits, and his efforts on behalf of African people:

> His plans were made known to them as soon as he was satisfied that the assemblage could be confided in, which conclusion he was not long in finding, for with few exceptions the whole of these were fugitive slaves.

Assembled here in Chatham in 1858 are the brothers that Malcolm would speak of in 1963. These are Malcolm's "field Negroes" (he called them "field nigga's." These are the brothers, Malcolm said, who when the Master got sick prayed he would die, when the house caught fire, prayed for a strong wind. When you said, "run away from here, let's separate, let's emigrate," they didn't question why, they simply asked: "which way?" Malcolm noted, "There were always more field Negroes than there were Negroes in the house."

It is field Negroes — fugitives, runaways, emigrationists, that John Brown is after: the only thing "house Negroes" (moral persuasionist, assimilationist, integrationist) can do is show him where the field Negroes are, and this is why he is in Canada.

"Rebirth" by students of Malachias Montoya, [Oakland,]
California College of Arts and Crafts, 1982. No longer extant.

Martin R. Delany, a brilliant and fiery spokes-
man for African rights. A Harvard student,
doctor, editor, world traveler, African explorer,
and scientist, he became a major in the Union
Army during the Civil War.

Martin Robison Delany, 1812-1885

Martin Delany, Black Nationalist and West Virginian! Martin Delany was born in
Charles Town in May of 1812 and became one of the most outspoken advocates for
African people. Calling us "**A Nation Within A Nation**," he believed our only salvation
lay in separation from America where we could exercise our potential to form a government, develop science, build institutions, initiate trade on a "world scale" and
properly take our place among the nations of the world.

Art by Jimica Akinloye Kenyatta (James Fisher)
United African American Artists of West Virginia

African Members of John Brown's Constitutional Convention of May 8, 1858 with Corresponding Black Conventions and Civil War Service

The following signators to the "Provisional Constitution and Ordinances for the People of the United States" were found with papers on John Brown's person when he and his men were captured. They were transcribed and published as part of the documents relating to the Senate investigation of the raid in 1860.

The Provisional Constitution was also signed by twelve white participants, including John Brown, details of whose participation are frequently included in histories. This is the first full publication of the African signators; Benjamin Quarles cited many in narrative form in Allies for Freedom (1974). Correlation with the Black Conventions, the African Commission (from Life and Public Services of Martin R. Delany by Frances Rollin), and Civil War service is ongoing research. Four of these men became elected officials in Reconstruction governments in the South.

Akin, George

Alexander, Robinson

Anderson, Osborn — National Convention of Colored Men 1869 (representing Michigan); Equal Rights League, 1865; Served in Civil War as recruiter and/or noncommissioned officer

Bailey, M.F. [Matisen, or Madison, F.] — African Commission, 1858

Bell, James M. [Madison] — African Commission, 1858; California, 1865

Cary, Thos. F. [died in 1861; husband of Mary Ann Shadd]

Connel, John — 113th U.S. Colored Infantry, Company A, private

Delany, M.R. [Martin R.] — Pennsylvania, 1843; Colored National Convention, 1848 Emigration Convention, 1854; Niger Valley Exploring Party, 1858; Major, 104th U.S. Colored Infantry, 1865; Sub-Assistant Commissioner, Freedmen's Bureau, South Carolina, 1865

Ditten, Stephen, alias Chitman

Ellsworth, Alfred M. — Illinois, 1853

Fisher, Simon — 1st Regiment U.S. Colored Infantry

Grant, J.C. [James C.]

Harris, J.H. [James Henry] — Ohio, 1856; African Commission, 1858;
   28th U.S. Colored Infantry, (Indiana) recruiter, possibly soldier;
   Equal Rights League 1865; National Convention of Colored Men 1869;
   North Carolina General Assembly, 1868

Hickerson, Thomas — 13th [poss. 113th] U.S. Colored Infantry, Company D,
   corporal

Hobbar, Isaac [Isaac Holden]

Hunton, S. [Squire, aka Esquire Hunter] — 109th Colored Infantry, Company
   H, commissary sergeant

Jackson, Job T. [John T.] — 123rd U.S. Colored Infantry, Company F, corporal

Jones, James M.

Kinnard, Thomas M. — Colored National Convention, 1855; 19th U.S.
   Colored Infantry?

Lambert, William — Michigan, 1843; African Mysteries, 1858; Equal Rights
   League 1865

Munroe, William Charles [or Munro] — Michigan, 1843

Newman, Robert

Purnell, James — Ohio, 1850,1851; African Commission, 1858;
   Pennsylvania, 1865

Reynolds, J.G. — Ohio Convention of Colored Men, 1858

Richardson, Richard — African Mysteries, 1858; 113th U.S. Colored Infantry,
   Company E, private

Shadd, I. D. [Isaac D.] — African Commission, 1858; Speaker of the House of
   Representatives, Mississippi, 1870-1871

Smith, Charles — 28th U.S. Colored Infantry, or 109th, or 127th (all include
   friends of John Brown and Osborne Anderson)

Smith, A. J. [Alfred J.] — 113th U.S. Colored Infantry, or 28th U.S. Colored
   Infantry

Smith, James — 113th U.S. Colored Infantry, private

Stringer, Thomas — National Convention of Colored Men, 1869;
   Mississippi Legislature, 1869

Thomas, John A. — Subterranean Pass Way, Massachusetts

Van Vruken, Robert

Whipper, Alfred — African Commission, 1858

REBELLIONS

The story of the African diaspora to the Americas is one of resistance and rebellion. It began on the slave ships to the European colonies, where so commonplace were ship revolts that the British created a special form of insturance to cover losses arising specifically from insurrections. Rebellions against slavery continued as uniformed units of the United States Colored Troops in the Civil War.

The successful African revolution that created the nation of Haiti had particular significance to communities of Africans in the United States, not only because of its success, but because of the communication of African culture and theology that accompanied it. Rebellion and religion were the twin elements that accompanied large insurrections.

There is great need of research on the role of the Mchawi (medicine manwoman/ herbalist/priest) who could bind people together along ideo-logical lines while planning and executing revolts. In Haiti, with Toussaint, it was Boukman. In Carolina with Vesey, it was Gullah Jack. There are ritu-alistic elements present with William Lambert and George De Baptiste of the African Mysteries in Detroit in 1860.

Jimica Akinloye Kenyatta

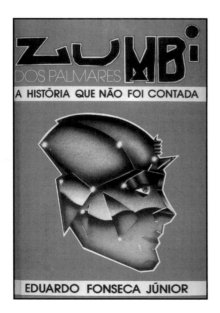

The African Brazilian nation of Palmares lasted a hundred years. It was a haven for fugitives and maroons. Iron artifacts have been found with ancient African processes.

"The General Plan Was Freedom:"
A Negro Secret Order on the Underground Railroad

by Katharine DuPre Lumpkin

in Phylon, The Atlanta University Review of Race and Culture,
Vol. XXVIII, No. 1, 1967.

Two ACCOUNTS OF a secret organization existing in Underground Railroad days have been found, both telling of an Order founded by free Negroes which was active in behalf of escaped slaves. The Order was called by several names: in one place, "African American Mysteries," and sometimes "Order of the Men of Oppression," and in another, "Order of Emigration." Like many episodes out of that strange time, this one is shrouded in a great deal of mystery . . . Yet in basic features the narratives agree that a secret organization was formed by free Negroes with the principal aim of aiding escaped slaves by conducting them from bondage into free territory; that the Order operated for a decade or more; that men were initiated by elaborate ritual, and some became conductors on the Underground Railroad; that its membership was large and admitted few whites; and that it bore some relation to John Brown's plan to bring freedom somehow to slaves of the South.

The two documents are interviews with William Lambert and George De Baptiste of Detroit in the Detroit *Post*, May 15, 1870, and Detroit *Tribune*, January 16, 1886. [*Both men are associated with John Brown; Lambert was an important leader in the Black Convention Movement and member of John Brown's Constitutional Convention in Chatham, Canada, in May, 1858.*]

William Lambert, a tailor, was educated by a Negro schoolmaster who was also an abolitionist and a Quaker. He was not long in gaining recognition, both as a public speaker and as fluent with his pen. He helped to form a Colored Vigilant Committee, and its work was well advanced by late 1842 . . . . The Detroit *Advertiser* of January 31, 1843 expressed astonishment at a petition from this organization: " . . . a document which would be creditable to any gentleman in this city, for its good sense and good taste, was written by Wm. Lambert, a young Negro of unmixed blood, in the employ of Robert Bank, another colored man."

George De Baptiste, like Lambert, was well-known. Trained as a barber, he became a bodyservant for various wealthy men, including General William Henry Harrison, remaining with him into White House days. When President Harrison died, De

Baptiste returned to Indiana and there began his career as an Underground Railroad agent. His house was a station on the Underground Railroad. The route he described is plainly seen on Siebert's detailed map of the Underground Railroad. From the accounts, we gain a picture of De Baptiste as a bold, ingenious man, courageous and thoroughly devoted to his cause.

At his death in 1875, the *Detroit Tribune* gave a column and a half to its notice of De Baptiste . . . he remained prosperous throughout his life, first as part owner of a barber shop, then of a bakery, and then of a steamship line than ran between Detroit and Sandusky on the lake . . . It told of how he raised a colored regiment in Michigan for the war, accompanying it to South Carolina; and was president of the Negro Union League of New York.

Order of Degrees of the African American Mysteries

Three degrees were named in both accounts: "Captives," "Redeemed," "Chosen,"and within the first degree a special step, this one called "Confidence," designed especially for agents of the Underground. Lambert's ritual gave an oath that fugitives were taught and a test they must respond to as they were moved along on the Underground line.

The Grand Lodge of the Order was located in Detroit. Lambert was precise about where the building stood: " . . . on Jefferson Avenue, between Bates and Randolph, about where No. 202 now is." The fugitives were brought from Wayne and Ann Arbor, arriving near the Lodge in the dead of night. They and all those with them went through the "test," and then were taken to the rendezvous, usually the house of J.G. Reynolds, another Negro agent in the Detroit area.

One of John Brown's company, George B. Gill, kept a diary: "Object in wishing to see Mr. Reynolds, who was a colored man (very little colored, however) was in regard to a military organization which, I had understood, was in existence among the colored people. He assured me that such was a fact, and that its ramifications extended through most, or nearly all, the slave states. He himself, I think, had been through many of the slave states visiting and organizing."

In 1860, Richard Realf testified that John Brown had expected Negroes to be his soldiers, and not alone slaves, although John Brown believed slaves would rise against their masters and join him in the mountains. According to Lambert, Richard Realf had been a member, one of the few white men ever admitted to the Order's highest degrees.

Historical Authors

Katharine DuPre Lumpkin
(Courtesy Wells College
Archives, Louis Jefferson
Long Library, Aurora,
New York)

Dr. Martin Luther King, Jr., recommended that the children of slaves and the children of slaveholders sit down together to make a better world. Katharine DuPre Lumpkin, sociology professor at Wells College in Aurora, New York, was born in Georgia, the daughter of a former Confederate officer and slaveholder. She became radicalized at the Bryn Mawr Southern Summer School for Women Workers in the 1930s. She studied labor in the South, and was published by International Publishers in New York: *The South in Progress,* in 1940. Her studies unequivocally showed discrimination toward Africans in occupational advancement, and a larger use of black children in southern industries. Then Prof. Lumpkin in 1967 documented the African Mysteries, the self-defense organization among free Africans, two members of which signed John Brown's 1858 *Provisional Constitution and Ordinances.*

The daughter of former slaves, Edna Christian Knapper of Chambersburg was awarded a citation for distinguished citizenship from the Pennsylvania House of Representatives at the age of ninety-one, in 1994. A lifetime teacher (beginning in 1912 in Delaware), she wrote of Joseph Richard Winters, whom she knew as a child at St. James A.M.E. Church. Mrs. Knapper researched property records as well as hearing the story from Winters' daughter of her father's arrangement of the secret meeting between John Brown, Frederick Douglass, John Kagi, and Shields Green in August, 1859. It was contributed to the editor by Mrs. Knapper in 1978.

Edna Christian Knapper
(Courtesy Kittochtinny
Historical Society,
Chambersburg,
Pennsylvania)

Outstanding Colored Citizens of Chambersburg — Past and Present: Joe Winters

By Edna Christian Knapper

[Chambersburg] *Public Opinion,* January 17, 1954

In the history of any community there are often those whose contributions to its growth and well-being have gone unnoticed and unsung. This is, indeed, a time of progress, of looking forward. But it is well to look back occasionally, and pay tribute to those who over the years have made possible many of the privileges which we now enjoy.

One of the most unique and versatile characters was Joseph Richard Winters, who, according to his autobiography, was born in Leesburg, Virginia, on August 29, 1816. His great-great grandfather on his father's side was the son of Chief Okichanconough, who was a frontier war warrior from 1636 until 1648, when he was shot in the back after he was taken prisoner by the English. His father, James Winters, was a brickmaker and made the brick for the gun works at Harpers Ferry. He died in Alexandria, Virginia, at the age of 103.

His grandmother on his mother's side was a daughter of the Shawnee tribe of Indians known as Half Kings. She was born in Waterford, Virginia, in 1767 and died in Chambersburg in 1864. She was known as "Aunt" Betsy Cross, the "Indian Doctor Woman." His mother, Aunt Betsy's daughter, married James Winters.

When young Winters was four years old he went to Waterford to live with his grandparents. In the meantime his parents moved from Leesburg to Harpers Ferry. On a visit to his parents, they refused to allow him to return to Waterford. Instead they put him to work sanding molds at the brickyard. The family moved to several places — to Halltown, Charlestown (on the farm on which John Brown was later hanged), to Shepherdstown, and finally to Chambersburg on Nov. 14, 1830.

Mr. Winters was tall, raw-boned with distinctly Indian features. He wore his hair shoulder-length and even in old age retained an erect carriage. Benjamin Need of the Kittochtinny Historical Society wrote: "He was called Indian Dick. He was intelligent, well versed in nature lore, and quite inventive." (Volume 7)

Since it has been established that Indian Dick was free-born, one can readily understand his interest and connection with the John Brown movement. By means of the "grapevine" Mr. Winters was advised of the real identity of John Brown, though he visited Chambersburg incognito. It was Winters who arranged the meeting between the famed Fred Douglass and John Brown, the meeting place and old stone quarry in West Washington Street, near the present Harbrough Poultry Market. It is believed that Winters had much to do with Brown's final decision to take the fatal step which led to the Harpers Ferry insurrection.

Mr. Winters acquired considerable property, the first purchase being two lots bought of Peter Swails and wife on August 1853, for the sum of $400 . . . The second purchase was made in July, 1856 for the sum of $300 from Conrad Warner and extended as far south as Catherine Street . . . The third and last purchase was made in October, 1872, the purchase price being $275. This plot of ground was located in what was then known as Wolfstown, and extended on from Loudon Street on the north to the Conococheague Creek on the south. (Deed book 52, page 108)

The story of Mr. Winters would not be complete without the story of his most outstanding achievement, namely, the invention of a fire escape ladder and hose conductor for which he obtained a patent from the United States Patent Office on May 18, 1882. An old picture taken of the invention in operation on South Main Street shows the ladder attached to the Montgomery House in North Main Street, a guest being lowered in a basket and Mr. Winters himself directing the operation. The ladder, an improvement over an English invention of 1866, was simple, inexpensive, occupied little space, was durable, easily manipulated and could not be tampered with without sounding an alarm. The patent, presumably protected, a company was formed known as the Winters Fire Apparatus Company, under the laws of the state of New York. Shares were sold at $100 each. After many trips to New York in a fruitless effort to raise capital for the manufacture of his invention and thus protect the patent, Winters returned home, a disappointed and disillusioned man.

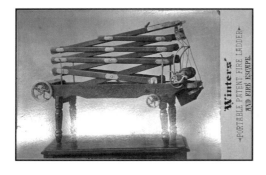

Though Mr. Winters received no pecuniary returns for his labor this in no way detracts from the staure of the man nor from his inventive genius. The manufacture of fire equipment has been protected, but as is often the case wth true genius, others have built on the foundation that has been laid by the early pioneers.

John Brown, Frederick Douglass, and Shields Green

I HAVE BECOME an intense student of the life of Frederick Douglass. He is a fascinating man, considering his personal history. It begins being born into slavery, escaping at a young age, and rising to become an orator and writer, diplomat and ambassador, and advisor to presidents and political leaders nationally and internationally. In reading his last autobiography, *Life and Times of Frederick Douglass,* I became fascinated by the man he writes of named Shields Green.

"SHIELDS GREEN": A strong, noble and dramatic name. He was also known as "Emperor," and sometimes "Emperor of New York." Benjamin Quarles wrote that the nickname " . . . could have come from the self-confident manner with which he bore himself; or perhaps from the rumor that he was the son of an African prince who had been sold into slavery." Imagine my disappointment in learning from further reading of Quarles that Shield's real name was "Esau Brown," having changed it upon escaping slavery in Charleston, South Carolina!! Nevertheless, the magic of the name had already been cemented.

John Brown met Shields Green while Brown was at Douglass's home in Rochester, New York in 1858, writing his Provisional Constitution. Brown briefed Green on his general plan toward combating slavery, and Green expressed enthusiasm in joining him. Quarles wrote in *Allies for Freedom* that Green was the first African American to be recruited for Harper's Ferry.

Brown wrote to Douglass in August 1859, several weeks before his planned raid on Harper's Ferry. Brown intimated in his letter that " . . . a beginning in his work would soon be made . . . ," and that he wanted to meet secretly with Douglass at an old stone quarry in Chambersburg, Pennsylvania, where Brown had moved and was living incognito. (Chambersburg is about 50 miles from Harpers Ferry.)

Brown asked Douglass to bring as much money as he could gather; in addition, Brown requested that Douglass bring Shields Green. It is proposed that Douglass did not know of Brown's plan to conduct a raid. If that were true, it is unlikely Douglass would have gone to Chambersburg.

Douglass and Green journeyed, with a stop in New York City to gather funds for Brown. Upon arrival, they contacted Henry Watson, an African

Lerone Bennett, Jr. "John Brown: God's Angry Man." *Ebony*, Vol. 20, no. 2, December 1964

(American) barber, and who was active in the anti-slavery movement in that area. Watson took Douglass and Green to the rendezvous, where they found Brown disguised as a fisherman. Brown had a price on his head, and was usually well-armed and suspicious of strangers. Already there at the hideaway with Brown was John Kagi, who was the Secretary of War under Brown's Provisional Constitution. Watson then left the stone quarry.

According to Douglass: "Our talk was long and earnest; we spent the most of Saturday and a part of Sunday in this debate — Brown for Harper's Ferry, and I against it — he for striking a blow which should instantly rouse the country, and I for the policy of gradually and unaccountably drawing off the slaves to the mountains, as at first suggested and proposed by him."[1]

The raid proposed by Brown constituted a marked change from the plan he originally proposed in 1858, and the change was the crux of their discussion. Douglass, an orator, and experienced in debate; and Brown, persuasive and direct. Two strong men intellectually, with different styles and means toward a common end; one wanting to hasten the pace toward overturning slavery; the other proposing a slower pace, and perhaps with fewer risks and greater chances of success.

There is no indication in Douglass's autobiography or in other sources that the discussion was bitter. As I reflected on this meeting from the very beginning, there was the suspense of learning what Shields Green was going to do, after listening to the debate. I gave no thought to Kagi; his actually being in Chambersburg with Brown was clear indication that he knew about the plan to attack Harper's Ferry, and was prepared to follow that plan. In fact, Kagi had been instructed to establish early residence in Chambersburg to assist in intelligence gathering and receive shipments for the raid.

Brown's concluding appeal adds to the drama of the occasion, and is testimony of the respect Brown had for Douglass. Douglass writes that in parting, Brown " . . . put his arms around him in a manner more than friendly and said: 'Come with me, Douglass; I will defend you with my life. I want you for a special purpose. When I strike, the bees will begin to swarm, and I shall want you to help hive them.'"

The bees Brown refers to is a metaphor for the slaves. Brown really wanted Douglass — not to be just a participant in the raid —but to serve as a beacon for slaves to run away from plantations and, hopefully, to join the Brown forces.

---

1. *Life and Times of Frederick Douglass*, 1893.

According to Douglass, when he was about to take leave, he turned to Shields Green and asked " . . . what he had decided to do, and was surprised by his (Green's) coolly saying in his broken way: 'I b'leve I'll go wid de ole man.'" Shields Green's response was immediate, simple — and brave.

At this point, it needs to be reported that Douglass had no fear of battle. He felt that for slaves to feel fully free from slavery they must fight for it on equal terms, and alongside others against the Confederate army and slaveholders. He was adamant in this position in discussions with Abraham Lincoln, finally getting limited endorsement of the idea from the President for enlistment of Free Blacks in the Union Army. Nevertheless, the raid on Harpers Ferry, as planned and described by Brown, was suicidal, in Douglass's view. This was a solemn moment. It was the last time he saw these three remarkable men. Douglass returned home to New York. The details and unfortunate results of the two-day raid on Harper's Ferry are elsewhere in this volume.

There is one aspect of the raid that must be recounted, however, and it pertains to Shields Green. During the early hours of the raid, Shields Green, Lewis Leary, Osborne Anderson, and three white raiders were sent out by Brown, as planned, to bring in freed slaves and their slaveholders as hostages from the surrounding area. Anderson and the white raiders returned with the hostages, but Green and Leary continued through the countryside, "hiving the bees." While away on this detail all night, troops began to surround the area occupied by Brown and his men. Seeing this entrapment upon returning to Harper's Ferry, Green met Anderson, and had an opportunity to remain under cover. Anderson did escape, and later met with Douglass. When he asked Anderson why Shields Green did not leave with him, Green told Anderson that he " . . . must go down to de ole man."

At the young age of 23, but obviously every bit a man, Shields Green, along with John Copeland, Jr. (a free man), John Cook, and Edwin Coppoc (the latter two white) were hanged October 16, 1859, fourteen days after John Brown was hanged. John Kagi and Lewis Leary died during the raid, leading some of the freed slaves that Shields Green and Leary brought in from the surrounding area.

Of the four men who met secretly at the stone quarry that day and a half in August, Douglass was the only one who became primary recorder of that remarkable meeting.

Long before the words became fashionable in the contemporary jargon of heroism, Douglass wrote of Shields Green: "John Brown saw at once what 'stuff' Green . . . was made of . . . ."

I concur.

Looking for John Brown

Each person has a John Brown to examine, whether inside or outside the pale of chronology, historical interpretation, and the textbook. He is a lightning rod in and of America. For Africans in America, John Brown is more relative to the entire history of slavery, and the way in which that is relative to the individual of African descent, than the historical quality of documentation, since that documentation was usually not created by Africans. How can a deliberately Africentric presentation qualify the documents, understand the process, when mostly written from without?

The presentation here is based first upon what John Brown wrote, which was to gain self-determination for people of African descent just as that of the raid on Harpers Ferry, Virginia. "I will carry the war into Africa," he said after losing the battle in Osawatomie, Kansas, in 1856. He planned to carry it for the people to manage.

Next are primary sources (eyewitnesses) that have been combed again with an eye for the local, ordinary person who is suddenly faced with history unfolding and who may not get out alive. Who saw that person, where were they? Are there at least two independent eyewitnesses? Is contradiction primary, or later interpretation? As John Brown said to those who felt slaves would not support him because they were cowards: "You have not read them right!"

Third, the references of recommended reading. These are more than the factual base, or secondary sources. They are what scholars are saying about the African center of American history. Most reference the important areas of Brown's life and work: the Underground Railroad, the creation of self-determining communities of living, of worship and fellowship, of equality, of family, and the value of hard work, well done.

Finally, we go places to look for John Brown ourselves, beginning at Harpers Ferry, to San Francisco, to Chatham, Canada West, then travel the Internet for sources and places to continue what is always personal journey into *sasa*, the African past and the African present, which is the same dimension.

Charlestown, Va., 2.ᵈ December, 1859.

I John Brown am now quite certain that the crimes of this guilty land; will never be purged away; but with Blood. I had as I now think: vainly flattered myself that without very much bloodshed; it might be done.

What Did John Brown Write?

In January, 1858, John Brown wrote a *Provisional Constitution and Ordinances for the People of the United States*, which was passed by the Chatham Convention and printed by William Howard Day in leaflet form. In it the organization for a traveling and armed (including women) group was set, government and rules of conduct specified. Many of the leaflets were found in the engine house at Harpers Ferry at Brown's capture, intended for distribution to those who agreed to join him.

Whereas, slavery throughout its entire existence in the United States, is none other than a most barbarous, unprovoked, and unjustifiable war of one portion of its citizens upon another portion, the only conditions of which are perpetual imprisonment and hopeless servitude or absolute extermination; in utter disregard and violation of those eternal and self-evident truths set forth in our Declaration of Independence: Therefore

We, citizens of the United States, and the Oppressed People, who, by a recent decision of the Supreme Court are declared to have no rights which the White Man is bound to respect; together with all other people degraded by the laws thereof, Do, for the time being ordain and establish ourselves, the following PROVISIONAL CONSTITUTION AND ORDINANCES, the better to protect our Persons, Property, Lives, and Liberties, and to govern our actions.

In January, 1859, John Brown directed the rescue of twelve slaves in Missouri (one was born on the escape). A second party, under Aaron Stevens, killed a resisting slaveholder in his house. Under criticism even from freestate abolitionists in Kansas, he wrote *"John Brown's Parallels,"* comparing the rescue with a massacre at the Marais de Cygne by unpunished proslavery forces. It was published first in the [Lawrence] *Tribune*, and taken up by other newspapers, including the [New York] *Tribune*.

Not one year ago eleven quiet citizens of this neighborhood [names them] were gathered up from their work and their homes by an armed force . . . were formed into one line, and all but one shot, five killed and five wounded . . . The only crime charged against them was that of being free-state men . . . . On Sunday, December 19, a negro man called jim came over the river to the Osage settlement, from Missouri, and stated that he, together with his wife, two children, and another negro man, was to be sold within a day or two, and begged for help to get away . . . Eleven persons [the rescued slaves] are forcibly restored to their natural and inalienable rights, with but one man killed, and "all hell is stirred from beneath."

(Courtesy John Brown Anti-Klan Committee, San Francisco)

Union is Strength: Nothing so charms the American people as personal bravery . . . Be firm, determined, and cool, but let it be understood that you are not to be driven to desperation without making it an awful dear job to others as well as to you. A lasso might be applied to a slave-catcher for once with good effect. Hold on to your weapons and never be persuaded to have them far away from you. Stand by one another, and by your friends, while a drop of blood remains; and be hanged, if you must, but tell no tales out of school. Make no confession.

John Brown's Final Address to the Court
November 2, 1859

I have, may it please the court, a few words to say.

Had I interfered in the manner which I admit, and which I admit has been fairly proved — for I admire the truthfulness and candor of the greater portion of the witnesses who have testified in this case — had I so interfered in behalf of the rich, the powerful, the intelligent, the so called great, or in the behalf of any of their friends, either father, mother, brother, sister, wife, or children, or any of that class, and suffered and sacrificed what I have in this interference, it would have been all right. Every man in this court would have deemed it an act worthy of reward rather than punishment.

This court acknowledges, too, as I suppose, the validity of the law of God. I see a book kissed, which I suppose to be the Bible, or at least the New Testament, which teaches me that all things whatsoever I would that men should do to me, I should do even so to them. It teaches me, further, to remember them that are in bonds as bound with them. I endeavored to act up to the instruction. I say I am yet too young to understand that God is any respecter of persons. I believe that to have interfered as I have done, as I have always freely admitted I have done, in behalf of his despised poor, I did not wrong but right. Now, if it is deemed necessary that I should forfeit my life for the furtherance of the ends of justice, and mingle my blood further with the blood of my children and with the blood of millions in this slave country whose rights are disregarded by wicked, cruel, and unjust enactments, I say let it be done.

Diego Rivera plaster fresco, "Pan American Unity" (1940), City College of San Francisco

Primary Sources

John Brown's Friends, Collectors of his Letters and Documents for Historical Memorial

Osborne P. Anderson, *A Voice From Harper's Ferry; by one of the number.* Boston: 1861, n.p. Anderson's account, by the only person on Brown's side who escaped and was not captured, has been reprinted in microform and in *Black Voices From Harper's Ferry.*

Life and Times of Frederick Douglass, 1893.

Richard Hinton, *John Brown and His Men,* first published in 1894, reissued by Arno Press in 1968. Hinton was one of the planners of the raid, and was nearby in Maryland when the event occurred. The Appendix reprints The Provisional Constitution, League of Gileadites and Kansas jayhawker bands agreements, Old Brown's Parallels, and an autobiographical letter written to a young son of George Stearns.

James Redpath, editor, *The Public Life of Captain John Brown,* 1861. Redpath was an abolitionist journalist who supported militant emigration and revolution by Africans, with Brown in Kansas. Unindexed and unchronological.

Franklin Sanborn, editor, *Life and Letters of John Brown, Liberator of Kansas and Martyr of Virginia.* 1885. Sanborn was one of the "Secret Six" white abolitionists in New England who funded Brown.

Frances Rollin, *Life and Public Services of Martin R. Delany,* 1868, 1883.

About the Raid, Collections of Newspaper Accounts, Reports, the Trial

The Insurrection at Harper's Ferry, 17th October, 1859. Document Y printed by the Maryland Senate March 2, 1860. The B&O telegraphs. Not reprinted, very hard to find.

36th Congress, Report of Committees No. 278. *The Select Committee of the Senate appointed to inquire into the late invasion and seizure of the public property . . .* June 15, 1860. Reprinted.

Stiverson, Gregory A. *In Readiness to Every Duty Assigned: The Frederick Militia and John Brown's Raid on Harper's Ferry, October 17, 1859.* Lost report of Colonel Edward Shriver, found at the Maryland State Archives and published in 1991.

The Life, Trial, and Execution of Captain John Brown, known as "Old Brown of Osawatomie; with a full account of the attempted Insurrection at Harper's Ferry, Robert M. DeWitt, publisher, 1859, reprinted by Negro Universities Press, 1969.

Richard D. Webb, editor. *The Life and Letters of Captain John Brown, who was executed at Charlestown, Virginia, Dec. 2, 1859, for an armed attack on American Slavery.* 1861, reprinted by Negro Universities Press, 1972.

Richard Zittle, compiler. *A Correct History of the John Brown Invasion at Harper's Ferry, West. Va., October 17, 1859.* Published in 1905 in Hagerstown, Maryland, has the stories in local newspaper, the *Sheperdstown Register,* of which Zittle was editor.

Boyd Stutler Collection. A vast array of materials collected over many years, purchased from his estate by the state of West Virginia and housed at West Virginia University in Morgantown. Published on eight reels of microfilm by Ohio State University.

Places to Go

LOOKING FOR JOHN BROWN is anchored in Harpers Ferry, the town which forever is burned by the lightning rod of his revolution. It stops time, a National Historical Park restored to be as it looked in 1859. A million pairs of feet on the cobblestones cannot hush sudden attention of the tracks as they begin to reverberate, carrying commuters, carrying freight, and the sighs of the men who stood outside and told the frightened passengers that they longed for liberty, or the black baggage-master, Haywood Shepherd, who didn't stop when told to "halt!", perhaps, like his white counterpart, because he did not know what it meant.

Is John Brown here, amidst the bustle of shops and living history lectures, the sight of the confluence of the rivers, and the ghosts of the Confederate defenders? Can an Africentric group visit Harpers Ferry and find John Brown, or do we feel discomfort, as Mrs. Edna Christian Knapper said, "like a Rebel was peeping around the corner waiting to shoot at me!"

The efforts of the National Park Service for the past twenty-five years to include African American history are evident. A display, "Black Voices From Harpers Ferry," is a permanent audiovisual record of ordinary people who lived in Harpers Ferry and Bolivar in what would become extraordinary times: Joseph Blanham, a free boatman who served time in prison for aiding fugitives; Johnson Garrett and Joseph Gust, who were underpaid "2000 or 3000$" for their work at the armory in the 1830s. There is a rare recording of the voice of the late Professor Benjamin Quarles addressing an interested group, and the presence of the mighty William Edward Burghardt DuBois, who protested a monument that limited the African participation to five.

Come on up to Storer College, opened in 1867 for the freedmen and for American Indians, restored to reflect a time when it was the educational cornerstone of the African community. Visit the Freewill Baptist Church, where convocations and services still resound with African American tradition.

Say hello to the Park Service people, who strive to make an experience for everyone to remember in an historically accurate manner.

Travel over to Charles Town, to the courthouse, where the words of John Brown's Final Address to the Court on December 2, 1859 can be read in the room where he spoke them, restored to its 1859 appearance. Visit the library, where in the basement is John Brown's wagon, the one that carried him to his execution as he looked around in amazement: "This is a beautiful country! I had not had the chance to see it before."

Then make your way to the African heart of Charles Town, Lawrence Street, to see St. Philip's Episcopal Church, built and attended by local slaves, and Wainright Baptist Church, where the stories of John Brown and local people were remembered for more than a hundred years. You'll want to look at the plaque on a building known as Fishermen's Hall, an 1890 meeting place of the fraternal United Galilean League of Fishermen. It is now being restored to be an African American Community Center. Then look at Star Lodge #1, the Masonic building, where African nationalist Martin R. Delany is on a plaque, dedicated in ceremony by the N.A.A.C.P. on August 7, 1999.

Drive across the Potomac to find John Brown's headquarters. See it from outside or, for a tour, contact Captain South T. Lynn, jbrown1859@aol.com. The Kennedy Farmhouse is at 2406 Chestnut Grove Road in the historic area of Samples Manor.

JEAN LIBBY, 1998

The farmhouse Brown rented across the Potomac in Washington County, Maryland, is restored to reflect the residence of John Brown, his daughter Annie, and the liberation army.

Meeting on a Train, 1976

IT WAS THE Bicentennial, a time to look for America, to return to old homes, to decide at age thirty-five what the next portion could be. Amtrak celebrated with a month-long pass — all you could travel, $250; children eleven and under, half of that. My accoutrements were three children, then aged thirteen, eleven, and five, a 4 × 5 view camera, and a determination to illustrate the epic poem by Stephen Vincent Benet, *John Brown's Body*. It was the final week of our 10,000 miles, and the three children were behaving as normally as any at such an interval, so I looked back across the aisle and saw this kind-looking man, and decided to change my seat for an hour.

We were on the Hudson River route, just back from Syracuse, and the gentleman was almost home. He was a European, an artist who lived in the Woodstock colony. As we talked, I told him about looking for John Brown, and he told me that he had painted some murals in the Rincon Post Office in San Francisco, in 1946 — had I seen them, living near there? – and that he painted John Brown from behind, being hanged, as one of them. A polit-ical attempt was made to remove the murals in the 1950s because of his support of the 1930s waterfront strike in another panel, and showing persecution of the Chinese, but they were saved and declared a city land-mark through the efforts of the late Emmy Lou Packard.

I called the Landmarks Com-mission after the Refregier murals were restored, suggesting they change "Vigilante Days" to an accu-rate description of the execution of John Brown. After all, I met the artist himself on a train, and he told me so.

Anton Refregier
Artist, 1905-1979

Three years after our train journey, October 12, 1979, in the *San Francisco Chronicle*: "Anton Refregier, Rincon Annex Muralist Dies." He was in his native Russia (his father was French), but his ashes were returned to Woodstock, New York, for burial. The newspaper included the panel of John Brown's execution, the pikes in the hands of the jurors looking away, armed workers running in front of John Brown's fort, Edmund Ruffin (slavery and states rights advocate in the Confederacy who committed suicide when the North won) holding a derringer shooting Abraham Lincoln (not noticing the cannon aimed at secessionists). They call it a "California vigilante execution."

Edmund Ruffin

Chatham, Canada West

NESTLED DEEP IN southwestern Ontario, just far enough from the Great Lakes and the Detroit River to be out of range of slave catchers, John Brown found a relatively affluent community of blacks. In Chatham, (now Chatham-Kent) Ontario in the 1850s, Brown found black doctors, professionals, merchants, farmers, and skilled tradesmen.

Brown visited Chatham in May 1858 in an effort to recruit former slaves for his attack on Harpers Ferry. Today visitors to Chatham can visit the First Baptist Church where Brown held two of his meetings. The church is now known as the "Old John Brown Meeting House" and an Ontario Heritage Foundation Plaque stands outside on the front lawn to commemorate the famous convention. The first meeting, however, was held in a frame cottage on Princess Street when he mislead people into thinking they were organizing a Masonic lodge of colored people (the first Prince Hall lodge formed in Canada in 1847). Some meetings took place in No. 3 engine house built by colored men.

Just a few steps away, on the property owned by convention delegate and poet James Madison Bell, is a plaque which commemorates Mary Ann Shadd Cary, editor of the *Provincial Freeman*. At the Woodstock Institute Sertoma Help Centre, 177 King Street, Shadd's descendant Gwen Robinson presents a slide show of Brown's convention, which includes portraits of the distinguished-looking delegates, including Dr. Martin R. Delany. She narrates the slide show as if she were at the convention, perhaps hiding in the pews. Ms. Robinson is passionate about Chatham's history.

Mary Anderson
(Courtesy Ava Speese Day)

There are many artifacts of Brown, and a portrait of Osborne Perry Anderson. This photo is of his cousin, Mary Anderson, who married Alfred Smith, another delegate of the convention. Many of the Chatham settlers, such as the Smiths, remained in Canada after the Civil War in the United States, forming the nucleus of the historically-minded community that exists among their descendants today. *Erica Phillips*

Erica Phillips is a freelance journalist, researcher, editor, and photographer based just outside Toronto, Canada. Holding bachelor's and Master's degrees, her continued academic commitment is to Black history in Canada, especially the Black press. Her main interest is promoting and preserving Black history in Canada as *Canadian history*. Erica responded to a query to scholars posted on H-AfAm, the Humanities Net academic forum on African Americans, on John Brown. She drove to Chatham and interviewed Gwen Robinson, who maintains the Heritage Center and tells the story of John Brown's convention to visitors. Erica Phillips has been published in several journals, including *Essence*. She studies at York University under the guidance of the Africanist Frank Lovejoy.

Henry P. Organ is a civil rights activist in California, dating from the 1960s and 1970s, when he arrived from Texas. He was active in public and private pre-education on the San Francisco mid-peninsula area (San Mateo County, and Santa Clara County, north of what is now called Silicon Valley). He chaired mid-peninsula chapters of the Catholic Interracial Council (CIC), and the Congress of Racial Equality (CORE). Henry Organ frequently contributes articles to area newspapers on problems of racial discrimination in employment and housing. Of late, he has developed an interest in, and written in opposition to, capital punishment. He developed an interest in Shields Green and the choice posed by John Brown, which Green answered affirmatively, while studying Frederick Douglass's life and works.

Judith Grevious Cephas is the daughter of a Virginia minister who moved to New York and worked with Adam Clayton Powell, Sr. and Jr., ordained at the Abysinnia Baptist Church. Judie was thus born in "Da Bronx," and proud of it. She is a Gifted and Talented Research Teacher at Paxutent Valley Middle School in Howard County, Maryland, and holds a Master's degree in educational technology from Howard University. She has been a member of Shiloh Baptist Church in Washington, D.C. (Carter G. Woodson's church) since 1985, and in 1997 received a fellowship from the Council for Basic Education to research Frances E.W. Harper.

Jean Libby is a writer and photographer, and an instructor of African and American History classes in community colleges in northern California. She has published *Black Voices From Harpers Ferry* (1979), *From Slavery to Salvation: The Autobiography of Rev. Thomas W. Henry of the A.M.E. Church* (1994), and several magazine articles on John Brown. Her honors thesis in African American Studies at the University of California, Berkeley, was an educational videotape: *Mean To Be Free: John Brown's Black Nation Campaign* (1986, with Roy Thomas). Her organizational affiliations are the American Studies Association (California chapter) and the San Francisco African American Historical and Cultural Society on the west coast, and on the east coast, the Friends of the Western Maryland Room at the Washington County Free Library, the Friends of the Catonsville Room at the Baltimore County Public Library, and the Harpers Ferry Historical Association. Jean has recently provided the identities in "Kansas Free State Battery, 1856" daguerreotype as those of John Brown's men.

Evelyn M.E. Taylor was "born and reared in Jefferson County, West Virginia." The daughter of the late pastor of the House of Prayer Church of God, Evelyn is an ordained missionary who has worked in southern Asia and eastern Canada. She has bachelor's and Master's degrees in the field of education. Evelyn Taylor is an administrator at the Brookings Institution in Washington, D.C., chair of the Historic Landmarks Commission in Charles Town; the author of *Historical Digest of Jefferson County, West Virginia's African American Congregations, 1859-1994* (1999). Her research for this volume took her to elder relatives in Jefferson County and Baltimore, as well as the deeds and wills that document the progress of the people.

Evelyn is an author whose writings, especially in early African American church history and its absence of historical documentation, rely heavily on the oral tradition.

James Fisher (Jimica Akinloye Kenyatta) is from the "free state of McDowell County", West Virginia. He is a veteran of the last Buffalo soldiers unit, 24th Infantry Regiment, in the Korean War. Moving to Brooklyn from 1954 to 1967, Jim joined the African nationalist Pioneer Movement, an offshoot of Marcus Garvey's United Negro Improvement Association. Settling then in Charlottesville, Virginia, he was president of the local NAACP and founder and director of New Birth Community Workshop. When James Fisher came to eastern panhandle of West Virginia in 1980, he joined the Carter G. Woodson Historical Association formed by Robert Davis and the late John Williams. He designed the cover and Martin Delany illustrations for *John Brown Mysteries*, is a member of the United African American Artists of West Virginia, the Jefferson County African American Community Association, and organizes the annual Storer College section of the African American Arts and Heritage Academy for youth.

Hannah Geffert grew up in the LaMott section of Philadelphia, named for Lucretia Mott, the abolitionist leader who operated a stop on the Underground Railroad and welcomed Mrs. Brown on the way to see her husband in Virginia before his execution. After graduating from Temple University, Hannah worked for the Lawyers Committee for Civil Rights Under Law in Washington D.C., and at the Antioch Law School. Her specialization in civil rights law took her to Florida, where she assisted migrant farm workers writing *Voices From the Field* to document their stories. She moved to "wild, wonderful West Virginia" in 1980, and is an instructor in Political Science, specializing in Black History and Oral History. She is the author of *An Annotated Narrative of the African-American Community in Jefferson County, West Virginia*, 1992. Hannah Geffert's paper on African American participation in John Brown's raid presented at a conference on John Brown in Mont Alto, Pennsylvania, in 1996 will be in a forthcoming volume edited by Peggy Russo and Paul Finkelman, published by the University of North Carolina Press. She is an active member of the Alliance for the Collection, Preservation, and Dissemination of West Virginia's Black History.

Louis S. Diggs is the historian of African American communities in Baltimore County, the author of three books and numerous exhibitions and lectures on the early settlements of both enslaved and free Africans. After dropping out of Douglass High School in Baltimore, he joined the all Black Maryland National Guard, which went to Korea in 1950 as the 726th Transportation Truck Company. During his military career he journeyed to Winters Lane in Catonsville and began learning family histories, as well as marrying a local resident, Shirley Washington. Returning to school, he earned an AA degree in 1976 at Catonsville Community College, then quickly garnered higher degrees at the University of Baltimore. Louis is fluent in genealogical research techniques, and has a grant from Baltimore County to develop community historical materials.

Eva Slezak is the developer of the African American collection at the Enoch Pratt Free Library in Baltimore, a task undertaken more than twenty years ago. She grew up in Oxford, Pennsylvania, near Lincoln University, an historically black institution, and is now a Baltimorean. Among her numerous published articles is "The Name is the Game, but not always the Same: Baltimore City Directories, 1796-1964" in *Flower of the Forest; Black Genealogical Journal*, 1983. Eva Slezak also writes and publishes the *Czech & Slovak Heritage Newsletter of Maryland*. Her interests lie in discovering patterns of history, communicating research needs, and connecting people with similar interests. To research her original map of Baltimore Centers of African Communities, 1859, Eva took her lunch hours and walked the vastly changed downtown areas of the early churches and communities; with photographer Monroe Frederick she traced the 1870 route of the 15th Amendment Celebration parade in Baltimore.

Acknowledgements

JEAN LIBBY, 1978

This is the arch under the Chesapeake and Ohio Canal used by Osborne Anderson to escape from Harpers Ferry on the night of October 17, 1859. The man portraying Anderson in this 1978 photograph is Rev. Albert Moser, then a student pastor serving the Asbury United Methodist Church in Shepherdstown. He moved to Washington, D.C., where he served two historic black congregations, St. Paul in Oxon Hill, Maryland, and Mt. Zion. His liberation theology included support of the antiapartheid movement among clergy in Washington during the 1980s. Today Rev. Moser is in the Clinton, Maryland, United Methodist Church, an ethnically diverse congregation. His mission is to continue to educate on equal determination and respect for all, and to make a difference in stopping the escalation of hate groups. The arch was located by the archivist of the Western Maryland Room, John C. Frye, by examining Osborne Anderson's account and relating it to the C & O Canal, which is a National Historic Park.

THE FIRST ACKNOWLEDGEMENTS for this publication go out to the souls of those departed — who have flown to Angola — since

Mrs. Dora Washington, a member of Asbury United Methodist church and the West Virginia NAACP, opened her home in Shepherdstown in 1978 to further this research. She assisted members of Allies for Freedom and others in their historical research on community history, emphasizing accuracy and commitment. This photograph was taken in 1988; she is sorely missed since her passing in 1990.

JEAN LIBBY

beginning this research study in 1976, those who informed and who trusted that the information would be prepared in such a manner that it would take a place in the John Brown literature.

Mrs. Mary Campbell Newman of Charles Town, and her father Donald Campbell, directed and accompanied the editor in this quest in the winter of 1977. Mrs. Dora Washington, Mrs. Effie Dennis Allen, Miss Charlotte Lovett, Professor John Wesley Harris of Jefferson County contributed to this research; as did Mrs. Marie Claybon, Mrs. Pearl Matthews, Rev. Leonard W. Curlin, and Miss Viola Steward in Maryland; Mrs. Edna Knapper, Mrs. Mary Jane Kauffman, and Mrs. Evelyn Chase in Chambersburg; African American scholar Dr. Paul Hardy at Solano Community College; the artist Anton Refregier of Moscow and Woodstock; John Williams, founder of the Carter G. Woodson Historical Association in West Virginia; the African philosopher and scholar, Dr. St. Clair Drake. These are the ancestors of *John Brown Mysteries*.

Any work that began nearly a quarter of a century ago, and involving this number of contributors, will have more acknowledgement due than can be properly applied. This attempt now credits those specific individuals who give *John Brown Mysteries* its substance. Hannah Geffert would like to thank our interview sources: Mr. Charles Cephas, Jr., Mrs. Lucille Woodland Cephas; and at Shepherd College, Dr. Mark Snell, Director of the George Tyler Moore Civil War Center; at Harpers Ferry NPS interpreter Eric Johnson. Eva Slezak and Jean Libby would like to thank the Rev. Frank M. Reid of Bethel A.M.E. Church on Druid Avenue; Ms. Slezak also especially credits Mr. Leroy Graham and Mr. Monroe Frederick of Baltimore for her work. Evelyn M.E. Taylor would like to thank Mrs. Florence Newman Brown, Mr. James Taylor, Mr. Russell Roper, Mr. James Surkamp, Rev. Walter A. Jackson in Jefferson County, and Mr. Thomas Newman in Baltimore, for interviews; Jean Libby wishes to thank Bishop Walter A. Newman of the House of Prayer, Church of God, James Tolbert of St. Philips Episcopal Church, and Jefferson County Prosecuting Attorney Michael D. Thompson in Charles Town, and Mrs. Elaine Gray of Baltimore. Erica Phillips expresses appreciation to Ms. Gwen Robinson of the W.I.S.H. Centre in Chatham for her historical presentation; Judith Cephas and Jean Libby would like to thank Dr. Gail Lowe, curator at the Anacostia Museum for her resource interviews and encouragement of their work.

Historical resource persons begin in Ontario, Canada for Erica Phillips with Professors Sheldon Taylor and Robin Winks; to Wells College in

with Professors Sheldon Taylor and Robin Winks; to Wells College in
Aurora, New York, Helen Bergamo, archivist, and Professor Leslie Martin-
Bernal, chair of Sociology, for finding Professor Lumpkin; to New York
City, James Huffman in Prints and Photographs at the Schomburg Center;
in Chambersburg, Murray Kaufmann and Mrs. Marjory Blubaugh at the
Coyle Free Library; in Hagerstown, Marsha Fuller and John Frye, archivist
at the Washington County Free Library; Park Service Interpreters Gwen
Roper, Melinda Day, Sue Baker, and William Banks in Harpers Ferry; li-
brarian Julie DeMatteis and Lisa Vicari in Catonsville; Civil War historian
Dennis E. Frye in Sharpsburg; National Firearms Museum curator Doug
Wicklund in Fairfax; library specialist Rhonda L. Williams in Fayetteville;
student and musician Jason McGill, now at Brown University; Dr. Edward
C. Papenfuse, archivist of Maryland; and in California, Marlene
DiGiovanni of the San Mateo County Geneaological Society, Dr. Susheel
Bibbs of the University of California, attorney Thomas Libby of Alameda
County; Clare Libby Loops, who designed the City College library with a
space for Diego Rivera's John Brown; the reference staff at the Palo Alto
City Library, and Jean Pauline at the Labor History Archives in San
Francisco. Librarian Ralph Libby contributed proof editing and research, as
he has for all the John Brown, African, and American history publications
that have lived in his house in Palo Alto, California, for nearly forty years.

Public information efforts are underway by Sandra Jowers and
Associates of Washington, D.C., assisted by Beth Libby and Stan Armstrong
of Armstrong Productions in Las Vegas, Nevada, and Dr. Joe Feagin of the
University of Florida. Many teachers around the country are spreading the
news of this nonprofit publication.

Graphic preparation is a major portion of this book. The authors
would like to thank Lisa Dillon of Shepherd College and the artists who
contributed: Josh Macphee, Tim Johnson, and Dennis Frye. Stan Cohen at
Pictorial Histories Publishing Company in Montana deserves much credit
for making this project come alive and be recognized with his *John Brown:
"The Thundering Voice of Jehovah"* published earlier this year. Without his
respect for historical photographs as primary sources, and that of Richard
Kassebaum of Kenner Films, who introduced us as pictorial resource persons for an "American Experience" biography of Brown that will be aired
on PBS, the images in this book would still be in file boxes. The graphic vi-
sion of Scott Perry of Archetype in Berkeley, California, brings the process
of digital imaging into the old slides and prints, which take us back in time
into the present, the African *sasa*.

Recommended Reading

These are sources we used to develop the factual and philosopical base of the mysteries, including collections of primary source documents not directly related to John Brown's raid. "Local histories" may be hard to find. Patronize your local bookstores, online Africentric networks, and ask your librarian for assistance with interlibrary loan! Photocopies of articles in journals are easily obtained this way. Or, for individual research guidance, email allies7@AlliesforFreedom.org.

Aptheker, Herbert. *American Negro Slave Revolts.* 50th Anniversary Edition, International Publishers, 1993. *To Be Free; Studies in American Negro History,* International Publishers, 1992. The historical base for revolutionary actions of enslaved Africans in America, paperbacks.

Berlin, Ira, Barbara J. Fields, et al. *Free at Last: A Documentary History of Slavery, Freedom, and the Civil War.* Documents by and about Africans to survive as well as gain emancipation: "the destruction of slavery was accomplished through black self-determination," states the *Journal of American History* in reviewing this book. The New Press, 1992, hardbound.

The Black Conventions. Several books of the *Proceedings* of State and National Organizations from the 1830s to the 1870s are in academic libraries. Look them up under editors, Howard Holman Bell, or Philip Foner. They contain resolutions and lists of delegates by region, county, or city.

Blackett, R.J.M., editor. *Thomas Morris Chester, Black Civil War Correspondent.* Biographical essay on the only African newspaper reporter in the Civil War, and his dispatches from the Virginia front, battles of 38th, 127th, USCT. Louisiana State University Press, 1991, paperback.

Blassingame, John W. "The Recruitment of Negro Troops in Maryland." *Maryland Historical Magazine,* v. 58, no. 1, March, 1963.

Blockson, Charles L. *The Underground Railroad; First-person Narratives of Escapes to Freedom in the North.* Modern, documented, indexed history that includes much on John Brown and the western emigrationists, the African Mysteries. Prentice Hall, 1987, hardbound.

Bracey, John H., August Meier, and Elliott Rudwick. *Black Nationalism in America.* Several writings and speeches of Henry McNeal Turner. Bobbs-Merrill, 1970, hardbound.

Brandt, Nat. *The Town That Started the Civil War.* Militant rescue of fugitive John Price in Oberlin brings John Brown to look for recruits; finds Leary, Copeland, Shields Green. Book ends in Harpers Ferry. Dell, 1991, paperback.

Braxton-Secret, Jeannette. *Finding your African Ameripean Ancestor in the Civil War.* Author's ancestor was in the Navy, joining as "contraband" when Admiral Farragut was on the Mississippi River. How-to for all branches of service. Heritage Books, 1997.

Britt, William H. *Retrieving the Past (1842-1997).* Madison Avenue Presbyterian Church, Baltimore, 1997, paperback (local history).

Carbone, Elisa. *Stealing Freedom.* Young adult book of research on the UGRR, the story of Maria Weems. Map of route from Unity, Maryland to Chatham, Canada West. Knopf, 1998, hardbound.

Clayton, Ralph. *Black Baltimore, 1820-1870.* Heritage Books, 1987.

Clinton, Catherine. *Civil War Stories.* Women and children, primarily in the Confederate states, including Frances Rollin Whipper (a South Carolinian). Biographical, exciting, also describes strong internal assistance to orphans by Africans. University of Georgia Press, 1998, hardbound.

Cohen, Stan. *John Brown:"The Thundering Voice of Jehovah; A Pictorial Heritage.* Many primary sources, including photographs. Pictorial Histories, 1999.

Connelley, William Elsey. *John Brown.* The author was a Kansas historian, and biography is primarily of Brown's territorial warfare. Connelley credits Osborne Anderson with the "most reliable" account of the raid. Found in the Fisk University Negro Collection, reprinted by Books for Libraries Press in 1971, hardbound (local history).

Diggs, Louis S. *It All Started on Winters Lane.* A history of the black community in Catonsville, Maryland. 1995. *Holding on to Their Heritage.* A history of the black community of Bond Avenue in Reisterstown, Baltimore. 1996. *In Our Voices.* A history of the black communities of Cowdensville, Arbutus, Chatonnollee, the Oblate Sisters of Providence. 1998. (local histories) Paperbacks, supported by loan and sale by the Baltimore County Public Library, Catonsville.

Drake, St. Clair. *Black Folk Here and There; An Essay in History and Anthropology, Vols 1 and 2.* World history with its African center by the renowned sociologist and an originator of Black Studies as a discipline. Center for Afro-American Studies, University of California, Los Angeles, 1987 and 1990, paperbacks. *The Redemption of Africa and Black Religion.* Emigration, Ethiopianism, Ras Tafaris, and black missionaries to Africa. Third World Press, [1970] 1991.

Finkelman, Paul. *Dred Scott v. Sandford: A Brief History With Documents.* The opinions, newspaper accounts, response by Frederick Douglass, Lincoln-Douglas debates, maps. Bedford Books, 1997, paperback.

Franklin, John Hope. *Runaway Slaves.* Rebels on the Plantation. Runaway slaves as dominant phenomenon of resistance. Oxford, 1999, hardbound.

Fresco, Margaret. *Marriages and Deaths in St. Mary's County, Maryland 1660-1900.* Lists alphabetically by first name within slaveholding families. Ridge, Md., 1987, hardback (local history)

Fries, Stella M., Janet M. Gabler, and the Reverend C. Bernard Ruffin. *Some Chambersburg Roots: A Black Perspective.* A potpourri of vital materials from and about Africans in Chambersburg, Pennsylvania: 1980, paperback (local history).

Frye, Dennis E. "White Plumes and Cornstalks: Jefferson County Pre-war Militia, 1858-1861." *Magazine of the Jefferson County Historical Society,* v. 50, 1984.

Geffert, Hannah N. *An Annotated Narrative of the African-American Community in Jefferson County, West Virginia.* Jefferson County and Berkeley County branches of the NAACP, 1992, paperback (local history) *Voices From the Fields: An Oral History of Migrant Farmworkers.* Farmworker Justice Fund, 1981. *Oral History of Shepherd College (1991).*

Graham, Leroy. *Baltimore: The Nineteenth Century Black Capital.* Seminal research on leaders, their connections in churches and fraternal organizations. Africentric, documented. University Press of America, 1982, hardbound.

Images of Dignity: The Drawings of Charles White. Foreword by Harry Belafonte. Introduction by James Porter, commentary by Benjamin Horowitz. Drawings include more of Harriet Tubman and of John Brown. Ward Ritchie, 1965.

Jabara, Robert. *The Word: The Liberation Analects of Malcolm X.* Describes an African American national minority in conflict with Black Anglo-Americans, and places assimilation in a worldwide context of ethnic minorities, including Europeans. Clarity Press, 1992, paperback.

Jahn, Janheinz. *Munyo: The New African Culture.* If one wants to characterize African culture, one must not separate place and time. Grove Press, 1961.

Katz, William Loren. *The Black West.* All the style and spirit the West deserves, with an historical base. Good John Brown in Kansas. Seattle: Open Hand Publishing, 1987, hardbound. *Breaking the Chains: African American Slave Resistance.* Excellent graphic presentation, includes a militant Dred Scott and more John Brown history. Athenueum, 1990, hardound.

Libby, Jean, editor. *From Slavery to Salvation: The Autobiography of Rev. Thomas W. Henry of the A.M.E. Church.* Documentation, illustration, and interpretation of the recovered 1872 pamphlet. University Press of Mississippi, 1994, hardbound (local history). "John Brown's Maryland Farmhouse." Preservation and restoration of the Kennedy Farm, with John Frye. *Americana Magazine,* v. 7, no. 1, 1989. *Mean To Be Free: John Brown's Black Nation Campaign.* University of California Television and Recording Studio, 1986 (with Roy Thomas).

National Park Service, *Exploring a Common Past; Researching and Interpreting the Underground Railroad.* This is "how to" explore and develop sites on the UGRR, using material culture with historical methodology. Written for museums, local historians, field research and trips. NPS, 1998, paperback.

The Heritage of Blacks in North Carolina. Linda Simmons-Henry, Philip N. Henry, Carol M. Speas, editors. Excellent reference for all African American collections. The Delmar Company, 1990.

Oates, Stephen B. *To Purge This Land With Blood; a Biography of John Brown.* Basic biography, should begin any research study focusing on Brown and the raid. University of Massachusetts Press, 1984, paperback.

Palmer, Ronald D. "Western Pennsylvania and the United States Colored Troops in the Civil War." Westmoreland County Historical Society, Greensburg, PA, 1997. (local history)

Phillips, Christopher. *Freedom's Port; The African American Community of Baltimore, 1790-1860.* Baltimore's black population of 27,000 was more than 90% free in 1860 — history of churches, lodges, leaders, business development. University of Illinois Press, 1997, paperback.

Quarles, Benjamin. *Allies for Freedom; Blacks and John Brown.* The only history which puts Africans at the center of John Brown's plans. Oxford University Press, 1974, hardbound.

Redkey, Edwin S., editor. *A Grand Army of Black Men; Letters from African-American Soldiers in the Union Army, 1861-1865.* These are letters to the periodicals of the independent churches. Cambridge University Press, 1992.

Rhodes, Jane. *Mary Ann Shadd Cary.* Definitive biography of first African woman newspaper editor on the continent (Canada), Civil War recruiter. Shadd was directly involved with John Brown. Indiana University Press, 1998, hardbound.

Simmons-Henry, Linda and Linda Harris Edminsten. *Culture Town; Life in Raleigh's African American Communities.* Information on James Henry Harris, John Leary, Reconstruction legislators who were friends of John Brown. Raleigh Historic Districts Commission.

Smith, John David, editor. *John Brown; A biography by W.E.B. Du Bois.* This newest edition of the 1909 Africentric classic has a good introduction and primary documents added. M.E. Sharpe, 1997, paperback.

Smith, Merritt Roe. *Harpers Ferry Armory and the New Technology; The Challenge of Change.* The technological and political history of the object of Brown's raid. Cornell University Press, 1977, paperback.

St. Joseph's Society of the Sacred Heart. *The Josephites; a Century of Evangelization in the African American Communities.* Although Josephites missions began after the Civil War, earlier priest Father Tessier and African nuns from Haiti (Oblate sisters) were in Baltimore; builders of St. Xavier Church for black Catholic congregation. The Josephites, 1993, paperback (local history).

Stake, Virginia Ott. *John Brown in Chambersburg.* Excellent history of the ordnance station of the raid, and site of meeting with Frederick Douglass. Much on escape and recapture of several raiders, including sucessful escape of Osborne Anderson through Chambersburg. Franklin Country Heritage, 1977, paperback (local history).

Sterling, Dorothy. *The Making of an African American: Martin Robison Delany, 1812-1885.* Doubleday, 1971. Editor, *Speak Out in Thunder Tones; Letters and*

Other Writings by Black Northerners, 1787-1865. Includes many of the nationalists and emigrationists. Doubleday, 1973, hardbound.

Taylor, Evelyn M.E. *Historical Digest of Jefferson County West Virginia's African American Congregations 1859-1994*. Middle Atlantic Regional Press, 1999, paperback (local history).

Thompson, Robert Ferris. *Flash of the Spirit: African & Afro-American Art & Philosophy*. Five African civilizations — Yoruba, Kongo, Ejagham, Mande, and Cross River — have informed and are reflected in the traditions of black people in the United States, Cuba, Haiti, Trinidad, Mexico, Brazil, and other places in the New World. Vintage Books, 1983.

Tobin, Jaqueline L. and Raymond C. Dobard, Ph.D. *Hidden in Plain View; The Secret Story of Quilts and the Underground Railroad*. African symbols in community formation that the UGRR transmits, as well as fugitives from slavery. Essays by Cuesta Benberry, Floyd Coleman, and Maude Southwell Wahlman. Doubleday, 1999, hardbound.

Ullman, Victor. *Martin R. Delany, the Beginnings of Black Nationalism*. The authoritative scholarly source by a descendant of the Union general. Beacon Press, 1971.

Whyte, James H. "Maryland's Negro Regiments — How, Where They Served." *Civil War Times Illustrated* July, 1962:41-43.

Wilentz, Sean, editor. *David Walker's Appeal to the Coloured Citizens of the World*. This is the revolutionary book of 1828 to which John Brown donated funds to help republish in 1848, with Rev. Henry Garnet. New introduction, "The Mysteries of David Walker." Hill and Wang, 1995, paperback.

Williams, Robert W. *Negroes With Guns*. Armed self-defense in Monroe, North Carolina against the Ku Klux Klan in 1957 is often compared with John Brown and the League of Gileadites. This is the book artist Josh MacPhee read that inspired him to make the John Brown poster in this volume, which quotes Henry David Thoreau's "A Plea for Captain John Brown." Third World Press, 1973, hardbound.

Wills, David W. and Richard Newman, editors. *Black Apostles at Home and Abroad; Afro- Americans and the Christian Mission from the Revolution to Reconstruction*. Includes essays on Henry Highland Garnet, Daniel Payne, Daniel Coker, Lott Cary, all clergymen associated with Baltimore, the independent church, African redemption and emigration. G.K. Hall, 1982, hardbound.

Wind, James P. and James W. Lewis, editors. *American Congregations*. volume 1, Portraits of Twelve Religious Communities, includes "The Social History of the Bethel African Methodist Episcopal Church in Baltimore: The House of God and the Struggle for Freedom" by Lawrence Mamiya. University of Chicago Press, 1994, hardbound.

Winks, Robin W. *The Blacks in Canada: A History*. McGill-Queens University Press, Montreal and Kingston, 1997.

What's the WWW?

Allies for Freedom *www.AlliesforFreedom.org* Information, updates on this book.

New Abolition Society *www.newabolition.org* The New Abolitionist Society, a group of radical scholars, challenges the privileges of whiteness by seeking to change the institutions that reproduce these privleges: schools, jobs, housing markets, the criminal justice system. Supports the journal *Race Traitor* (a name frequently associated with John Brown). They will have John Brown Day activities around the country in May, 2000, as they did in May, 1999.

John Brown Portrait by Augustus Washington, African American Daguerreotypist *www.si.edu/activity/exhibits/npg.htm* An exhibit at the National Portrait Gallery in Washington, D.C., from September 24, 1999, to January 2, 2000, features the rediscovered 1847 portrait of John Brown holding a nationalist organization flag with his hand upraised.

Speak to My Heart: Communities of Faith and Contemporary African American Life *www.si.edu/organiza/museums/anacostia/speak/tour.htm* Don't miss this exhibit at the Arts & Industry building on the Capitol mall until May, 2000. It is also available online.

National Underground Railroad Freedom Center *www.undergroundrailroad.com* The Freedom Center is based in Cincinnati, the symbol of freedom for fugitives. Lectures by scholars James Oliver Horton, John Hope Franklin, online. Freedom walks information. Much good information about John Brown's role with the UGRR, a site to keep current.

Aboard the Underground Railroad; a National Travel Itinerary *www.cr.nps.gov/nr/underground/ugrrhome.htm* The National Park Service is putting much energy and funds to develop the Underground Railroad history because of the National Underground Railroad Act for site preservation by Congress in 1998. You can plan your trips with this one, with lots of background information. Begins with John Brown in Kansas.

Mary Ellen Pleasant, a Friend of John Brown *www.mepleasant.com* The Mother of Civil Rights in California assisted John Brown with funds and travel, escaping capture from southern Virginia when the raid failed. Researcher and lecturer Susheel Bibbs performs her life story at public showings, has books on many facets of the life of this enigmatic person.

Susheel Bibbs as
Mary Ellen Pleasant

Martin Delany Home Page *www.libraries.wva.edu/delany/home.htm* A collection of Delany's writings, time line, articles from "The Mystery," developed and maintained by Jim Surkamp of Shepherdstown for public distribution and dissemination.

Maryland State Archives *www.mdarchives.state.md.us/msa/refserv/html/findaid. html* Much related material on this site, including the research by David Troy on the celebration of the 15th Amendment in Baltimore, a complex lithograph that includes John Brown, Frederick Douglass, Martin Delany, Masonic marchers, USCT veterans.

Heritage Books, finding ancestors *www.heritagebooks.com/afr-am.htm* Heritage Books publishes geneaological works by family researchers; has many valuable offerings and older books in its catalog, may be ordered online. Includes the how-to books by Jeannette Braxton-Secret, and a complete compilation of the pension records of 83 soldiers recruited from plantations in the low country of South Carolina by Major Martin R. Delany of the 104th Infantry Regiment, by J. Raymond Gourdin.

Civil War Soldiers and Sailors System of the National Archives. *www.itd.nps.gov/ cwss/index.html* This is where we found the veterans of Maryland units and the Chatham Convention delegates. Search engine for the USCT by rank & unit.

Valley of the Shadow *jefferson.village.virginia.edu/vshadow2/choosepart.html* University of Virginia historian Edward L. Ayers, the faculty and students of the History Department, developed this site to show primary sources of two communities: Augusta County, Virginia, and Franklin County, Pennsylvania (which contains Chambersburg) in their relationship to the John Brown raid, the Civil War, and afterward.

"Pan American Unity" by Diego Rivera *www.riveramural.com* An interactive exhibit of the San Francisco mural, which includes John Brown teaching liberty.

Louis S. Diggs' Historical Page *www.min.net/~puma/ldiggs/* The Baltimore County expert has material online to get you to the African American settlements, a reenactor group honoring a forgotten Medal of Honor winner.

Baltimore County African American Cultural festival *www.min.net/puma/festival* The annual event in Towson, opening venue of *John Brown Mysteries* in 1999

African American Women Writers of the 19th Century *http://149.123.1.8/schomburg/writers_aa19/toc.html* A complete reproduction of Frances Rollin's *Life and Public Services of Major Martin R. Delany*, plus many others of interest.

Black Canadian History *www.pathsofglory.com* Resources for students and teachers; specifically for middle and secondary-age students, and useful for everyone.

Many Rivers to Cross: The African-Canadian Experience *http://citd.scar.utoronto.ca/Multi_history/blacks.Many_Rivers/TOC.ht. Excellent site curated by Sheldon Taylor.*

This lithograph was produced by E.B. & E.C. Kellogg of Hartford, Connecticut, in 1860. This unsigned depiction of Brown was intended for circulation among his supporters. Once initial condemnation of the Harpers Ferry attack changed to support by the Northern press, the brothers signed the lithographs. (Stan Cohen, *John Brown: "The Thundering Voice of Jehovah,"* 1999.) The original, which is in color, was photographed from the wall with a 4×5 Speed Graphic camera, Ektachrome film, at the restored headquarters of Stonewall Jackson in Harpers Ferry with permission of the owner, Mr. Newcomer, in 1976.